UNDER THE ORANGE BLOSSOMS

AN INSPIRATIONAL STORY OF BRAVERY AND STRENGTH

CINDY BENEZRA

Cindy Benezra/Under The Orange Blossoms
Printed in the United States of America

Under The Orange Blossoms/ Cindy Benezra -- 1st ed.

Publisher's Cataloging-in-Publication data
Names: Benezra, Cindy, author.
Title: Under The Orange Blossoms, an inspirational story of bravery and strength / Cindy Benezra.
Description: Kirkland, WA: Cindy Benezra, 2022.
Identifiers: LCCN: 2022903354 | ISBN: 979-8-477-87268-8 | 978-0-578-38047-6
Subjects: LCSH Benezra, Cindy--Mental health. | Adult child abuse victims--Biography. |
Adult child sexual abuse victims--Biography. | Post-traumatic stress disorder--Patients--
United States--Biography. | BISAC BIOGRAPHY & AUTOBIOGRAPHY / Personal Memoirs |
HEALTH & FITNESS / Mental Health | SELF-HELP / Abuse | SELF-HELP /
Post-Traumatic Stress Disorder (PTSD)
Classification: LCC HV6626.5 .B46 2022 | DDC 362.7/6/092--dc23

I dedicate this to you. To each and every being who has walked a similar path. There is light at the end of the tunnel. You are not alone.

AUTHOR NOTE

I have written about both my friends and family in this book. These memories are mine as I recall them and are my version of my past. They are in no way intended to harm anyone in this book.

FOREWORD

Under the Orange Blossoms is an astonishing debut. Cindy Benezra writes openly about the innate ability children have to survive early childhood trauma. She does so with incredible compassion, bravery, truth, advocacy, and love.

Cindy reveals her story of survival and coming of age trying to escape the post-traumatic stress she suffered at her father's hands. This is a story of hope—of finding your way out of the darkness and into the light.

She provides unique insight into the healing modalities and steps she used to help her survive, thrive, and create post-traumatic resilience despite her losses. It is a heartbreaking and heartwarming story of facing fears, dealing directly with pain, breaking cycles of generational trauma, and ultimately letting go of the anger and creating a beautiful life.

Cindy is living proof that you are not your abuse, trauma, or story. It's what happened to you, but it doesn't define you. Under the Orange Blossoms is a must read.

Angela Schellenberg, Writer, Speaker and Mental Health
Trauma Therapist, LMHCA

CHAPTER 1
SLICES OF SUNSHINE

"There are wounds that never show on the body that are
deeper and more hurtful than anything that bleeds."
-Laurell K. Hamilton

I pop a warm orange slice into my mouth and methodically eat it to distract myself from the pain. I notice the texture and sweetness. It tastes the way sunshine feels. Everything about oranges brings me a sense of calm. I've felt this way since I ran away to the orange orchards as a little girl. I read somewhere that an orange scent triggers happy endorphins. I'm living proof.

I stick my thumbnail into the orange rind, breathe in the bright, citrusy scent, and watch the ultra-fine spray be carried away by the balmy Mediterranean breeze. I sigh and release my hold on myself. I remember to breathe. Each time I break into the skin to peel it and expose the fleshy fruit, the spray permeates the air, leaving a slight residue of sticky nectar on my fingers and the floor below. I put another orange slice into my mouth and gaze at the horizon toward the sun. I've eaten oranges this way hundreds of times.

Since moving to Torremolinos, Spain, back in 1979, I've never missed a sunset. In fact, it has become a cherished family ritual. The best spot to take in the splendor is from our apartment balcony. Mom usually makes a brief appearance just before the sun dips below the horizon, and the world fades to black. For Sonya (my younger sister) and me, it's our new religion. We sit for hours like an old married couple without saying much, but there's no need; taking in the setting sun is monumental. While the sunset is an everyday occurrence, the Earth revolving on its axis and the sun's dramatic splashdown is nothing short of miraculous.

Today, I can't miss the sunset because I need to see something beautiful. Something to remind me that there is splendor in the world. Something to ground me in my body. I'm numb. Searching. Disconnected. I need to feel connected to something. I need a reason to wake up tomorrow. I need something to live for, such as the sunset that paints the sky in unexpected ways and makes you believe in the wonder of the universe.

I love my family, but they're not enough to drive away my troubling thoughts and dangerous impulses. I've thought this whole thing through. Jumping from my bedroom window five flights down onto the red terracotta tile floor with the pretty red, white, and blue mosaic tile in the center seems like the only way out—the only way to stop the pain. I imagine my body striking the ground like a giant sack of flour, making a heavy, echoing thud. Would my head explode like a sack of flour, too? The only problem is that I'm not crazy about messes or drama. I imagine the sweet gardener stuck with the cleanup after my limp body is hauled away. He would shake his head and say, "Que lastima," (what a shame) as he sprays down the sidewalk with pity. What's left of me gets washed away into the drainage ditches and out to the sea. I can't have anyone pitying me. No, I can't have that.

As I secretively sit on my bedroom windowsill, my legs dangling in my faded bellbottom jeans, I can feel the hemline hitting my bare feet in the breeze. I wear a flowy linen shirt embroidered with flowers. If I weren't so in my head, I would notice the view of the sea over red-tiled roofs and a tanker traversing the calm, sparkling water. I think of reasons why I should jump. *I can't live with the pain and nightmares stalking me.* Then I think of why I shouldn't jump. *It would break my mother's heart. It would devastate Sonya. I'd miss myself.* My dad doesn't cross my mind either way. I move my bottom a few inches closer to the edge and gaze down at the tile below. I wonder if I'd feel terror or physical pain before dying. The truth is it wouldn't be any worse than the emotional pain I live with every day. *But what if halfway down I change my mind, and it's too late?*

My shame is so intense that I entertain the thought of jumping to make the feelings go away. I do this daily for a while. I fear jumping, but I like the idea of all my memories going away instantaneously. I go through the steps of the foreseeable process of me jumping. One is that I would die instantly. Another is that I would survive and become a quadriplegic and live on life-support, trapped with my memories. Yet another is that I would have broken bones and a head injury then die from some horrible secondary infection. My mother always tells me so many people get secondary infections from being in hospitals, and she says that it is the worst way to go. I imagine this will probably happen to me, so I pivot my legs and bottom back through the window, step onto my bed pressed up against the window, and lie down to gather my thoughts. I realize I'm trembling from having come so close to the edge.

For months, I've been having horrifically disturbing nightmares—haunting and, unlike my usual surreal dreams, incredibly real. It's as if I see spliced-together film footage of things that really happened. *Is this what it feels like to go crazy?* I curl up in a ball, hugging my knees to my belly.

A new dream starts in the shadows like an opaque movie with occasional dialogue—with fragmented and scenes that are out of order. Through repetition, the dream becomes clear and seemingly whole. In the dream, I'm the observer, watching myself from above. I close my eyes, and my last dream replays, even though I will it not to.

In my bed in Arizona, at the age of five, I laid as still as possible, with my covers tucked around my chin. The curtains were cracked, and the glow from the streetlight cast eerie shadows onto the walls, like phantoms. The window was wide open, and the dry evening air carried the scent of chaparral into our room. The crickets sang to each other in a pulsing chorus.

I was hypervigilant; my ears perked up at every creak, shuffle, and whoosh. I realized the night speaks to you if you're willing to listen. The clinking of my dad's ice cubes against his glass helped me track him as he slunk around, drinking his bourbon. Clink, clink, I heard him in the living room. Clink, clink, in his office. Clink, clink, louder now, at our bedroom door. I could hardly breathe. Although I shared a room with Sonya, she slept through everything.

With my eyes squeezed shut, my mind raced. *Is he going to hug me and tell me how much he loves me? Is he going to spank me for doing something wrong? What could I have done wrong?* He approached my bed and tapped me several times, whispering in my ear with bourbon-scented words. The smell of alcohol on his breath made me queasy.

"Wake up. I want to teach you something. Shhh!"

I pretended to be asleep, but he persisted. He lifted me out of bed, and I quietly shadowed him to the living room. He was extra careful not to make a sound as we passed the bedroom where Mom was fast asleep. My dad pulled the bedroom door until it almost closed. I rubbed my sleepy eyes so I could see better in the dark hallway. I usually didn't like the dark, but with my dad leading me, I felt safe and protected from whatever might have lurked in the shadows.

The streetlights softly illuminated the living room. Full of curiosity, yet fatigued and just wanting to sleep, I sat next to my dad on the couch when he motioned for me.

With a strange smile and a hushed voice, he said, "I'm going to show you how to make yourself feel better and," he paused, "how to make me feel better."

I hadn't realized we needed to feel better.

"This is going to be so special that you can't tell a soul. This will help you be a better girl." His eyes locked onto mine. "And remember, this is our secret. Do you understand?"

I nodded. *Maybe being a better girl meant I wouldn't get into any more trouble. Maybe being a better girl meant I wouldn't get spanked for everything, like not picking up my dolls, making up silly songs, playing and jumping around. My dad would stop jerking my arm and shouting, "Come here!" in a heavy German accent. He'd stop spanking me until my bottom hurt so much, I couldn't sit down afterwards.*

"Stop! Stop! Stop!" I cry out to an empty room. I jerk awake, my eyes blinking in the darkness. My heart pounds, my mouth is parched, and I reach for a drink of water. I'm not a little girl, and Sonya is next to me, sleeping deeply. *It's just a dream,* I tell myself. I feel nauseous and disoriented, resisting my dream with all my might. *If it feels so real, then mustn't it be true?* But if it is, how could I forget such a traumatic incident? *Oh, I know. Maybe this is a past life thing.* This summer, I read a trippy book on past lives, claiming we carry our past lives in our consciousness and that life events can trigger memories from those lives.

Uhhh. I rub my head, trying to clear out the muck. *What's happening to me?* I'm so confused. I was living my life and then—whammo! I fell under a dark force's spell. Am I possessed or something? Who can I turn to for help? I can't share what's going on with Mom or Sonya because I don't trust anyone other than myself with my thoughts. Sonya is a tattletale. I don't have faith that she will keep my thoughts to herself. I understand her thinking, but I don't trust it. As for Mom, she would book me on the first flight to the States and check me into a psychiatric ward.

Am I just kind of crazy, or am I going off the deep end? How can I figure it out? It's not like I can go to a library and check out books to determine my state of crazy. I'm in Spain, for God's sake, and can't read Spanish! Maybe I came up with these dreams from reading disturbing stories. I just can't seem to remember. But it's weird that I'm in these dreams. I can't even trust my judgment right now. I was just sitting on my windowsill contemplating killing myself! The fact is that I'm overly cautious, but no one would ever know it. Everyone thinks I'm a light, happy, carefree fluffball, which I am, but I have a deep, complex side that I keep to myself. I don't like to show this side to anyone. Maybe if I keep it hidden, it will just go away. I'm a deep thinker for my age. People don't want to go there.

Once I was with friends waiting in line on a sidewalk while hundreds of ants scurried around our feet. I said to a friend, "I wonder what the ants are saying to each other."

My friend did a doubletake and shook her head. "That's just weird, Cindy." She turned her back on me and whispered to another friend.

I wanted to ask her, "Don't you wonder about the deeper side of the universe? I think not wondering is weird." But I said nothing and tried not to look at the ants.

Another time, when I was with my mom, we strolled by a guy clad in overhauls who was sawing a tree, its sap oozing out onto the bark. I said, "I wonder if it's hurting."

"You wonder if what's hurting?" Mom asked.

"The tree."

My mom pressed her fingers against her forehead. "You're a strange kid."

I have always wanted to be light and fit in, so I stopped sharing my deeper side, but that made me feel lonely.

My racing heart draws my attention to my tight chest. I gently massage my chest to dissipate the tension. My t-shirt is clammy, like the rest of me. I cup my forehead to see if I have a fever. "Nope, I'm just going crazy; that's all," I say to no one. My voice echoes in the tiny bedroom I share with my sister. Then I laugh like I do when I'm stressed. It helps me feel grounded in my belly. Laughing shakes up the tension and releases the tight, achy pit that grips my stomach. I fake-laugh again and again. "Hahaha! Hahaha!" I bellow. If anyone were witnessing this scene, they'd think I was Looney Tunes.

I picture a kitchen sifter—the kind I make cakes with. I bake when I'm stressed. I know that if I bake and give away sweet treats, I'll make someone happy. I pour flour into the sifter, pulling the handle back and forth until the flour funnels through it. The lumpy flour that goes through the sifter becomes soft and fluffy. "That's me!" I say out loud. "I'm soft and fluffy all over." Then I really start to laugh at the irony of me being light and fluffy. All the shit going into my sifter becomes light, fluffy shit, and I feel better. I really do. I smile at myself and think, *twisted humor for a desperate mind.*

I jump off the bed and head toward the balcony. On the way, I grab the wooden bowl of oranges and lemons from the dining room table. I plunk down on the balcony floor, leaning against the invitingly cool whitewashed wall. The terracotta tile warmed by the sun heats up my bottom. The black wrought-iron railing frames the azure sea off in the distance. A cute elderly couple slowly swims the breaststroke in the swimming pool below, while chatting and giggling. I'm not visible to people at street level, which is good because I don't want to see anyone or force myself into a conversation.

Mom, Sonya, and I have been living in Spain for a year, and I feel like a local now. Mom is so good about integrating us into this community so we can live as locals. We buy Spanish clothing. We shop in fresh veggie and fish markets, mingling with the locals, who love to practice their English.

Our fifth-floor apartment has two bedrooms. My sister and I share a tiny room furnished with two twin beds. The small but practical kitchen lacks a dishwasher, and the apartment doesn't come equipped with a washing machine or a dryer. Our entrance opens to a modest-sized living room and dining room. Everything is covered in marble, even most of the walls. Mom says it keeps the place cool in the summer, which is perfect, but the winters are freezing! The main room opens to a beautiful balcony with an unobstructed, panoramic view of the Mediterranean Sea. Mom created a beautiful garden of potted plants and flowers on the balcony. I spend most of my time there; it's the focal point of our apartment. It allows me to see who's swimming in the pool below and who's coming and going in the streets.

I admire the balcony's touches—the potted flowers, candles, and several sitting areas. Mom has a way of making things feel cozy and beautiful no matter where we live. I glance around at our neighbors' laundry flapping in the wind. Everyone hangs their freshly washed laundry out to dry on their balconies. Today, the theme is brilliantly colored dish towels and swimsuits. It adds to the charming beach life in Spain.

Mom pops her head out of the sliding glass door. "Oh, there you are. Why are you sitting on the floor?"

"The warm tile feels good. I'm just taking in the sunset and enjoying my orange. Do you want some?" I say, smiling and offering her an orange wedge.

"No thanks." She shields her eyes to look at the sun. "It'll be setting soon." Mom quickly admires her flowerpots, sits down at the deck table for four and props her lean brown legs on a chair, and then looks off into the distance.

Feeling emotionally rattled from the thought of taking my life, I hold up the large wooden bowl of oranges resting between my legs and stick my head deep into it, inhaling the oranges' scent. Immediately, I'm back in the orange grove in Arizona, and a sense of wellness washes over me.

Mom stares at me with a furrowed brow. "What in God's name are you doing? Cindy, that's weird. Here—give me one of those."

I get up and hand her an orange that she starts to peel. I plunk down. "What? It's perfectly normal to plunge your head into a bowl of oranges." I laugh sardonically. *Especially to prevent yourself from jumping off a balcony. She has no idea how normal sniffing oranges is compared to what I was just plotting.*

She shoots me a wry smile and rests her gaze on the expansive view.

I think it's weird that Mom wanted to move to Spain to speak her "native tongue," which is Spanish, but she's Mexican, so shouldn't we have moved to Mexico instead? I also think it's strange that she read *Don Quixote,* who traveled to the village of Torremolinos where we live now. She reads and rereads the book as though it's the most fascinating thing in the world. I think it's the most boring read ever, but that doesn't stop me from searching for windmills. Don Quixote famously battled a windmill here because he thought it was a ferocious giant. I haven't seen one windmill yet. Maybe Don Quixote had all the beasts removed.

My mom's not nearly as weird as her daughter. It's pathetic that I'm almost 17, want to hurt myself, and can't tell a soul. If I'm dead, I won't dream, and the pain will cease. Maybe it's not so weird, just a logical solution to an intractable problem. *Who wants to live in constant pain, haunted by nightmares?*

Sonya joins us on the balcony, plucks an orange out of the bowl, and sits next to me without saying a word. She's so close; I breathe in her sweet, earthy scent. Eau de Sonya. I watch the fiery sun set against the horizon of the dark blue Mediterranean Sea. The sun is a giant orange, plunging into the depths and signaling the end of summer. *Ugh!* I wish I could go back to boarding school in Austria when I felt strong and independent before the nightmares set in—before I no longer recognize myself.

My boarding school was in Lech, a charming tourist town that looked like a movie set with its rugged mountains and snowcapped peaks sloping down to lush green grassy hills. The Lech River meandered through the town with picturesque Austrian cottages and hotels with floral potted balconies. Being far from home without my parent's daily guidance helped me grow up quickly. I relied on my intuition and instruction from our teachers. When I traveled solo back and forth from Austria to Iran, where my parents lived, I did so without a cell phone. I had the address of my destination jotted down on a piece of paper, and crossed my fingers that plane, trains, and taxis would carry me there—and they did, as if I were on the wings of a magical bird.

Whereas before, I had slipped through the cracks in school; I was able to catch up academically and emotionally. I felt more carefree and discovered my voice without censorship. For the first time, I lived without fear of having to avoid others and found my own interests without my parents' influences. I learned how to calm myself when in conflict and love myself without Mom's hugs, gluing myself together with the love of those around me. I learned it was okay to struggle with not getting things right the first time. I developed faith that no matter what came my way, I would make it through.

I wish I could go back to *that* Cindy, the one without a care in the world, the one who felt she could conquer the world at 14. Sadly, *this* Cindy doesn't know who she is anymore and doesn't know how to find her way back.

CHAPTER 2
INHABITING TWO WORLDS

*Courage doesn't happen when you have all the answers. It happens when
you are ready to face the questions you have been avoiding your whole life.*
-Shannon L. Adler

As our chemistry instructor scribbles equations on the chalk-board, ones that we must know for our upcoming lab, my mind wanders. He keeps saying "net iconic equations," and I have no idea what it means. When he writes: $Ca(NO)(aq) + KOH$ (aq), I copy it down in my notebook. However, jotting things down on paper doesn't prevent my mind from drifting back to my life in Iran when Dad uprooted our family for his job.

I'm 13, standing in a pistachio field and listening to the birds while the wind rustles through the leaves of the trees. The moist, heavy scent of the earth fills my senses, and I wiggle my toes in the rich dirt. I stretch out my arms and feel the heat of the sun on them.

My friend, Raza, looks at me strangely and says, "What are you doing? Are you a tree?"

I smile quizzically. "I have no idea what I'm doing, but there's something magical about being in an orchard like this. Do you feel it, too?"

He hesitates and glances toward the house to see if anyone is looking. He kicks off his shoes and socks, and he then joins me. We clutch each other's outstretched arms to form a tree. He tilts his face towards the sun, and I blink my eyes closed. We stand in silence for the longest time until he laughs. "I've never done this before," he says.

"It's a good thing because it's kind of strange." I giggle and continue. "You know you are really lucky to inherit this pistachio farm."

His eyes widen. "I am?"

I wonder how he can't see it. *Maybe we always take for granted that which is familiar.*

Afterward, I went swimming with his sisters in the garden and reflected on the lovely serenity of my experience. The pistachio field felt so familiar, but I couldn't quite place it. It filled me with a sense of calm—a feeling that I am not alone. I felt that my higher power is present. I love it here. Moving to Iran has given me a fresh start. I feel stronger, more independent, and so removed from the dark days of Arizona. I'm healing, but from what, I don't know. *Does everyone have scars from secrets they can't remember?*

When the bell rings, I shake off my reverie and turn to my red-headed classmate, Tina. "It's lunchtime! Finally!"

"Yeah, I know. I'm starving, too!" she says, putting her hand on her belly.

Although I'm happy it's lunchtime, I'm not actually hungry. I just need someplace to go to process my thoughts and be with friends. I find a seat next to my friends in the cafeteria and shove my pate and tomato sandwich into my mouth. I don't even taste it. I swallow it in one gulp. I follow the rising and falling timbre of my friends' voices.

The boys wisecrack—flinging zingers and comebacks, laughing all the while. I'm amused by their ability to joke around and not take it personally. Girls don't really do that kind of a thing. We do it behind each other's backs—so wrong on so many levels.

My friend, Paul, swirls the ice in his glass to cool his Coke and takes a few sips, then swirls it again. Tom, who is dishing out the jokes, is doing the same thing with his glass.

Ugh! What's going on with the swirling? Stop it, already! For some reason, it makes me agitated and angry. I want to stop fixating on it, but I can't. I stop following the conversation because the *clink, clink, clink* of the ice against the glass has pulled me into another world. My stomach gurgles, my hands are clammy, and I'm overcome with the fear I felt as a little girl. At bedtime, it wasn't lullabies, lights out, and sweet dreams at my house. It was pure anticipatory terror. Minutes later, I hear nothing in the cafeteria but the sound of my driving heartbeat. *Can my friends hear it, too?* I try to calm myself, but my heartbeat throbs in my head. I think this might be the moment I go crazy. I wait for the crazy to take over. But it doesn't.

I heard my father's glass as he skulked around the house in the dark. *Is he coming to my room? Will he check on me and then walk away? Will he stand above my bed and watch me? Will he wake me?* The fear of not knowing gripped me. I was frozen in bed. *Go away! Please, please, please go away.* Pretending to make the same heavy sleep breathing sounds as my sister in the bed next to me, I hoped that it would keep him away. I was sweaty with fear. I prayed to God, wished on a star, and prayed to God again that he won't come into my room. Before my prayer was finished, my father shook my shoulder, whispering, "Wake up. I'm going to teach you something." I could hear my dad's voice as if he were sitting in the cafeteria next to me. I could smell his foul breath. My mind flashed, and my tiny hand was in my dad's sweaty hand, moving up and down his stiff pee-pee. Nausea and terror swirled in my stomach. *Is this what it means to be a good girl?*

My daydream cuts out to another.

I violently pushed my dad off me as he tried to jam his slimy tongue into my mouth. I could feel his tongue on my gums where I'd lost two baby teeth. I had put the teeth under my pillow one night to find two silver dollars the next morning. Mom wasn't home, so I ran out the front door.

I'm not sure how old I am in these dreams. *Dreams or memories? Memories or dreams?* They're jumbled together, and sometimes I'm five, ten, seven, and then five again.

My friends burst out in riotous laughter, and someone smacks the table, pulling me back into the cafeteria with the scent of coffee and fried food. I'm here and not in my daydream. I'm here and losing my mind. I feel sick to my stomach. I feel dirty and filled with so much shame. I need to wash myself, clean off the grime, the filth, the muck. But how? I announce to my friends that I'll be right back.

I step outside into the sunlight and hear the kids shouting and bouncing balls during recess. The carefree days of elementary school with jump roping, tag, hide-and-go-seek. I sit down on the steps and take a deep breath to cleanse the filth from the corners of my mind. For the first time, I notice my tears. Everyone was laughing so hard in the cafeteria; they were crying. I hope nobody noticed what was going on with me and thought my tears were ones of laughter, too. I heave a sigh of relief. *How can I explain what is going on with me to my friends? To anyone? I wouldn't even know where to begin.*

Two girls on the basketball court bounce a ball back and forth to each other, giggling and shrieking with delight. I am about their height in my dream. I stroll over to the basketball court and ask the girls how old they are. They both have brown hair in ponytails with ribbons and are as sweet as can be. They say with huge smiles that they are best friends. One is six, and the other one is five, about to be six. They show me their age with their fingers.

I return to the stairs, plunk down, and hold my head in my hands, thinking about being that age. I do the math. *I'm almost 17. So that dream, no, that memory, happened when I was five or six. These 11-year-old memories have been stored in my body just waiting for the right time to emerge. Why is this the right time? Can't I push the memories back down to their hiding place? Can't I go back to not remembering? Can't I reclaim my innocent childhood?*

After school, Sonya and I get off the bus and traipse up the long hill to our apartment without speaking. We are both tired from the day. It was a tough day to stay in my body. My dreams are too much for me to handle, and I want to space out and get lost in a daydream that has nothing to do with dads violating little girls. I want to spirit away to a place where children are sacred and safe. My imagination is so much kinder than the real world.

I heave open the dark brown, wooden carved door, walk in, and shout out into the emptiness of the hallway. "We're home!"

"Oh, is that you, kids? Hi!" Mom calls out from her bedroom.

"Who else would it be at the same time every day?" Sonya says sarcastically.

"Yeah, and who sounds like us?" I say only loud enough for Sonya to hear. "Mom, don't you believe in locking the door? It's always unlocked." I say, annoyed, and lock the door and go into the kitchen to see what's in the refrigerator. "Hmmm. Same old thing since this morning," and I frown at my sister.

"Oh, no, it's not! Looky, looky! He, he, he!" Sonya says as she pulls back a slew of jars covering several small bowls with saucers on top of them.

Mom says from her bedroom, "No. And don't eat the flan either."

"How did she know?" Sonya asks.

"She has eyes everywhere," I say. *Well, if Mom has eyes behind her head, why did she not know that Dad was coming into my room? She's so aware of things, but somehow, she's not.*

"So, was that no, you don't believe in locking doors, or no, don't eat the flan, or both?" I query Mom, walking into her bedroom, where I find her reading on top of her bed.

She pulls down her book to see me. "No, to all of the above," she retorts. "What's wrong?"

"Ohhh," I mutter as I plop myself next to her in bed and squish myself tightly against her in a side hug. My leg on top of hers and my arms around her waist, I bury my face into the side of her shoulder. "I had the worst day at school. I didn't want to be there, and I was spacing out all day, picturing being back in bed and getting one of your power hugs, too." I pause and the words just come out. "I'm having the worst nightmares, Mom," I say with heaviness.

Mom's book is propped up on her chest, but she puts her book down open-faced on the bed to keep her page and rolls slightly into me and says with concern in her eyes. "What are you dreaming about, and how long have you been having these dreams?"

"Off and on for some time, and I don't know how to make them stop. They are *the* worst dreams of being chased, and I'm running for my life! I mean running in terror! Most of the time, Dad's in them, and I want the dreams to be a lie. I wake up covered in sweat." I rub my face like I have sweat on it. I quickly bury my face back into her shoulder for comfort and welcome the safety of her soft, brown skin.

"Tell me more." Mom says in a hushed tone.

"I can't get into it, Mom." I barely whisper with despair but continue. "It hurts too much. I feel like I'm being tortured, and I don't know what's real. That part is the worst. I dream about me being in the old house in Phoenix, and I hate myself for dreaming these things."

Mom and I lie in silence. It feels so good to share a little. There's comfort in her concern and questions.

Mom asks, "Why your father?" There is a giant pause like the earth stands still.

Should I go into more detail and tell her everything? I'm afraid of her response. What if she locks me up in a mental ward, and they shove a bunch of medication down my throat and keep me in isolation, just like the movie, One Flew Over the Coocoo's Nest? I saw it a bunch of times. Drooling in isolation doesn't sound very therapeutic. I'll take my chances. What about electric shock therapy or a lobotomy? More silence passes.

19

Mom says with careful consideration, "Hmmm. Maybe you just need a good nap."

I think I feel my heart stop, and I wonder if I'm still breathing. I focus on my heartbeat, and suddenly, I hear the incredibly loud thumping. I feel cold and clammy. My mind screams, *Nooooo! Mom, you can't do this to me! Where's my nosy Mom who asks a thousand follow-up questions? The one who cares! The one that has eyes behind her head. How could you betray me like this? Your denial just told me it's all true! Who's in denial here, me or you? I love you so much yet hate this part of you! Don't leave me alone to figure this shit out on my own again. Please!*

If my heart physically could have shattered into a thousand shards of glass, it would have. I feel the silent pain of the shards as they burst through my rib cage and radiate through my body and out the bottom of my feet. I silently question, *Mom, where are you? Why can't you be the mom I want you to be in times like this? You betrayed me once and now again?*

Mom breaks the silence by moving back to her original position to read her book. She softly says, "I've been reading about Mary, Queen of Scots. Do you want to hear about her life? It's kind of like a soap opera. This will be good to take your mind off things."

I look at her and say, "Mom, I love you, but sometimes, I just hate you!"

Her mouth drops open with surprise.

"Who cares about Mary, Queen of Scots?" I exclaim, seething with disappointment. I scoot out of Mom's bed and head across the hallway into my room.

Mom yells, "Oh, come on, Cindy!"

I calmly close the door to block out the hurt. I plop onto my bed and close my eyes to process everything.

I turned the doorknob of our Arizona home ever so gently as I slipped out the back door. I stepped into my spare tennis shoes placed just outside the door, poised for a quick escape. I tied them on the fly, not wanting to waste a second of precious time. I scurried to the right side of the house, where I had recently parked my getaway vehicle— my bike—so it was ready to go when I needed to sneak out. I had rehearsed my escape many times in my mind's eye, realizing the best way to minimize my chances of being seen out the front windows was to pedal like crazy through the desert. Once I reached asphalt, I could release the hold on myself.

I swung my thin, bronzed leg over the long banana seat to straddle my bike and set my eyes on the desert path ahead of me. It was 1970, and I had just won a super cool banana-seat bike in an Easter drawing contest. Its frame was splashed with pink and purple, and a large, woven, white basket attached to the front held my snacks—the oranges and apples my mom gave me each day as I went out to play. The playing cards I'd attached to the spokes with clothespins made clicking sounds as the tires turned. Pink, white, and purple streamers flowed from the handles and blew chaotically in the wind as I pedaled. I loved the sensation of the streamers against my arms—the feeling of freedom. I felt I could go anywhere my bike would take me but especially away—far, far away.

My mouth quivered as I went, and I felt shaky all over. I steeled myself against my nerves, frantically pumping my legs past the front windows, hoping my parents wouldn't catch a glimpse of me doing what they had forbidden. Once I hit the dry, pale-hued dirt, I wove through the cacti to avoid puncturing my tires on their needles. I kept my eyes peeled for patches of jumping cholla cactus. Brushing up against their prickly spines would mean fragments lodged in my skin. However, I wondered if I would've felt anything given the adrenaline coursing through my body. I pedaled with all my might while carefully maneuvering the jagged path. As my tires spun from bumpy dirt to the smooth asphalt of the highway, I inhaled deeply. I realized I had been holding my breath the entire time.

The highway was the one place I was forbidden to go, but today, I didn't care. I knew if a neighbor had seen me, they'd tell my parents, and I'd be grounded, or worse, they could take away my bike—my freedom. None of that mattered today as I pedaled toward the orange blossoms.

Irrigation channels lined either side of the road, and the desert landscape was dotted with homes that backed up to the orchard off in the distance.

I pumped my bike pedals with all my strength until I felt like I was flying, but soon my legs began to cramp. In the safety of the highway and so close to my special place, it all came out, everything I had been holding in. Tears streamed down my cheeks and angled toward my ears, pooling there before dripping down toward the earth. But I couldn't stop, not even for tears. Not yet.

Once I reached the symmetrical rows of orange trees, I turned down a row and rode deep into the orchard so no one could see me. Pedaling over the dried, muddy berms, my bike dipped and rose so fast the oranges and apples I carried in my basket danced. The scorching desert sun zapped my energy, but I continued pumping the pedals with everything I had. Once I reached the fourth row, I ditched the bike and sprinted deeper into the orange grove. I ran until my burning legs wouldn't carry me any further. I threw myself down on a berm, buried my head in my arms, and sobbed—the kind of crying that leaves you breathless, the kind of crying that feels like it will never end.

The rustling of the orange tree leaves was so soothing. It felt like a blanket wrapped around me. The shadows of the leaves danced across my closed eyes. I could have stayed here forever, living off juicy oranges and sleeping on the warm earth beneath the blossoms, intoxicated by their aroma. Maybe it would help me forget.

I opened my eyes and sat up, questions flooding my mind. *How am I going to get out of this? Where am I going to go?* I couldn't talk to anyone, and the feeling of being trapped and uncertain of what to do triggered another surge of weeping. *It's okay. Only the trees are listening.* In the empty orchard, I let out a deep, guttural scream. Peering up at the sapphire sky, I shouted, "I hate you! I hate you! I hate you!" I stood up and kicked the edge of the muddy berm so hard. I should've felt my foot throbbing, but all I could feel were the disgust and anger lodged deep inside my gut. Every time I screamed, my pain was released into the trees around me, as if the branches were arms cradling me and the oranges were offerings of sweet grace. Even the dried-up, crusty berm I struck with my foot absorbed some of the pain.

When my foot was numb, I folded my legs beneath me and collapsed to the warm, hard earth. I closed my burning eyes, sensing the warm air around me and breathing in the intoxicating scent of the orange blossoms—the lingering sweet citrusy perfume. *This is what heaven must smell like.* I inhaled the pure fragrance deep into my belly, cleansing the disgust and anger trapped inside and filling me up with its beauty. With every breath, it calmed me. The heady mix of orange blossoms and exhaustion left me feeling still and centered.

I cradled my head in my palms, which rested on my knobby, ashy knees. A gust of earthen dampness emanated from below and spiraled up into the rustling leaves. I tuned into nature's symphony, which is so often drowned out by the noisy business of living.

Everything that I had carried was now among the trees of the orchard, and I was filled with the beauty around me. I lifted my head, which felt lighter than it had minutes ago, and slowly opened my eyes to see my red sandals and white bobby socks splattered with mud. *Uh oh. If my dad saw the mess I'd made, he'd go ballistic.*

I walked briskly to my bike and mounted it, suddenly aware of potential dangers that lurked in the empty orange fields. I was all alone in the grove, far from home, and no one knew where I'd gone. Not only that, but I also had taken a risk by biking on the freeway. With my heart racing again, I crossed the main road and rode back as swiftly as I had come. As I pedaled home, South Mountain darkened, offset by the blue and pink Arizona sky behind it. I would be late for dinner if I didn't pedal faster.

Since becoming a teen, I've been very respectful to Mom. She treats me kindly, so I do the same in return. It's rare that I just fly off the handle unless I'm PMSing. Mom chooses to live in denial at times.

Why? I don't know other than it must be easier. It's probably like my daydreaming. People call me Dreamy or Spacey Cindy. I check out mentally during the day when I'm bored or forced to listen to Dad rant and ramble on about nothing. I've always called it spacing out, daydreaming, or checking out, but I just learned the word for it: dissociation.

A disconnection or separation of something from something else or the state of being disconnected. In extreme cases, multiple personality disorder.

When I read about it in my health book, it nearly takes my breath away. The book covers other mental illnesses, but they don't register because I only focus on dissociation. There it is in black and white. I practically dissociate after reading the meaning, too!

Holy Hell! Am I like that girl in the movie, *Sybil*?! I never caught myself talking like a different person. Sometimes I speak with a fake Mexican accent, but I don't think that means I have a personality disorder. Or does it? No, Mom tells us to knock it off because it's disrespectful, and we stop instantly.

Dissociating is like a vacation to a place full of color with happy people and more interesting places. Everything is funny there, and sometimes I have magical powers. It's fantasy, and I can snap right into that world just as quickly as I can snap out of it.

A boy named Brad lived across the street from us in Arizona. He was autistic and a few years older than me. I'd go over to his house when I was hiding from Dad. We'd talk while he played with his toys, and eventually, he'd tire and mentally go into his own world instead of talking to me. I told him that I do the same thing when it gets tough for me with my father. He never looked at me when I told him, but I know he heard me because he interrupted me after a while and said, "I'm going now." He never left physically but spaced out into his world.

He asked me, "Are you there?" meaning, are you in your day-dreaming world?

I answered, "Yeah. My place is a silent place."

"Oh," he said, and continued to make random noises, paced, and said things that made no sense to me. He was in his world, and it was probably easier for him to be there. I completely got it, and he was the only person I shared with because I knew he would understand. He lived in another world like me when he wanted to because it was safer.

In Spain, at 17, when I move from one side to the other side of my twin bed, the familiar creaks of the bedsprings are comforting. I'm calm now and reach for my journal under the bed to write what just happened with Mom.

I open the journal to my last entry.

What there's to live for, and why I should stay? Are these the only choices? There's got to be a better way. Maybe there's another path. Maybe it's just time. Time will heal.

My mind is a battleground, and the pages reveal my battles. On these pages, I see split sides of my dilemma. One side of me wants to live in denial like nothing ever happened. I want to hold onto all the nice things and pretend I had a perfect childhood. I probably could choose to do that—but could I, really? Just block everything out and tell myself it's a lie like everyone wants me to do. That's what Mom does. She wants to live with the good things. She doesn't want to dwell on anything ugly; that's why she does this. Maybe it's a choice to live in denial. I think it's the cowardly path—neither real nor truthful. Eventually, the truth has to come out. Doesn't it?

One Thanksgiving, when we were kids, Mom prepared a beautiful dinner. Our family, including my aunt, gathered in the kitchen in anticipation of a mouth-watering meal. Mom asked Dad to turn the turkey. Resisting her simple request, he flew into a rage and violently stabbed the turkey with a large butcher knife. The bird slipped onto the floor with a loud splat. Trembling, he hacked up the turkey, shouting, "The turkey's done!" and then glared at my mother.

My mom picked up the turkey and put it back into the pan.

If the dreaded Thanksgiving ever comes up in conversation, Mom simply says, "It was a really good dinner. I remember my cranberries turned out so nice," as if she has amnesia.

I can't live like that, but if I acknowledge and accept that my dreams are real, then I do not want to live in this body. I want out. The pain, shame, and disgust inside me make me feel like I can't be loved. I feel so ugly all over. A hot bath and a nap can't wash this one away. *Really, Mom?!* The genie is out of the bottle, and I can't put it back in because I'm too fucking mad! That's why! I'm in a silent hell. I face the shattered fragments of unwilling memories barraging me throughout the day, when I should be living a carefree teenage existence. I hate my life! I hate myself! I might not have a choice but to soldier on until I can figure everything out.

CHAPTER 3
THE SILENT SCREAM

"As long as you keep secrets and suppress information, you are fundamentally at war with yourself... The critical issue is allowing yourself to know what you know. That takes an enormous amount of courage."
-Bessel A. Van Der Kolk

One day in high school, a girl named Sofia catches up with me as our fellow students rush through the hallways between class periods, chattering on the run.

I'm off to algebra, dreading the deadly boring activity of solving for x, y, and z.

"Hi, Cindy," she says, breathlessly.

"Oh. Hi, Sofia."

Sofia has unruly dark hair and intense black eyes with too much eyeliner, making her eyes look even more extreme than they already do. But maybe that's the point.

She grabs my arm and pulls me aside, as though she has something urgent to tell me.

"What's wrong?" I ask with concern.

Sofia leans in and whispers, "I heard a rumor that the boys think you're a cock tease."

"What? Me?" I ask incredulously.

She nods with grave concern. "They call you the queen of blue balls."

I can't help but laugh. "Okay. That's both ridiculous and hilarious."

But she clearly doesn't think so. "I thought you should know what they're saying behind your back."

"Hey—thanks for telling me." I stride toward algebra class, acting nonplussed about my cock tease reputation, but I peer into boys' eyes as I pass to see if I notice expressions of disdain or contempt. Most seem more concerned about themselves than the queen of blue balls.

Of course, I can't focus on the algebra teacher's lesson that day as he furiously scribbles equations on the chalkboard. Is there anything wrong with liking smart guys who enjoy deep conversations and can make me laugh? While all my friends are sexually active, I'm stuck at the kissing stage. I would happily stay there forever, but it seems to become a real teenager, you must take the plunge—especially in Spain. Unlike in the States, sex isn't a big thing; it's just a natural part of life. Being sexually active by 14 is the norm, and you don't even need a boyfriend. You can just hook up with anyone, at any time. I was hoping to fly under the radar and not stand out, but apparently, it's not working. Having turned 17 just a few weeks ago, I'm the oldest virgin in my grade.

I put off the inevitable as long as possible. I decide to put it off even longer by deliberating over who will help me lose my virginity. Friends advise me to look at shoe and hand size as an anatomical clue, which I think is hysterical. *Big-footed guys are better in bed?*

I plan a series of make-out sessions with different guys. It's all very calculated. While French-kissing, I stick my hands down their pants to assess their size. I think Alejandro, a guy with tiny hands, might be the one, but when I reach down and grab, I gasp. He's huge! Talk about false advertising! Despite my girlfriends' advice that the larger the penis, the better, I decide the right guy must have a medium-sized or even a small one. *No huge weapons, please.*

I scrutinize my classmates, not only for physical traits but also for personality. I examine their behaviors and interview the few boys who make the cut. Of course, they don't know I'm interviewing them. After much deliberation, I finally choose Mateo. He's a little older than me, good-looking, communicative, and kindhearted. And, most importantly, he has a micro-penis! I decide the setting will be a weekend party. I'll finally lose my virginity and discover what I've been missing. I imagine orange groves, lakes, and arcing rainbows. Paradise awaits.

I tell Mateo I'm a virgin, and he says, "We're all virgins to a new person!"

I'm not sure if he believes me, but he is very patient and accommodating, which are the most important things. Even though he knows what he's doing, he only lasts for a hot minute. "Minute Man," I think to myself. I hope it gets better. Afterwards, we hide behind our clothes, awkward about being naked with each other. It's nothing like *The Love Boat*. No fireworks.

I'm horrified to discover I stained the bed when my hymen broke. Although I feel incredibly embarrassed about the bedding, I'm really glad it's over. Embarrassed and relieved, I scurry to the bathroom to clean up. I check myself in the mirror to see if anything is different about me. *Nope, same Cindy. But, hey, I'm no longer a virgin! Hooray! Shouldn't I get a ribbon or a badge?* I laugh. *But what's with all the hype about sex? It was awkward and uncomfortable. I just don't get it.*

I date Mateo for a month, but I don't want to be tied down. However, when I meet an Argentinian guy named Eduardo, he gives me more freedom and independence than Mateo did. We waver because we're too young to be serious, but we truly enjoy each other's company. We sometimes fool around in bed, kissing, heavy petting, and sometimes more serious stuff, which I know I shouldn't be doing without protection.

In Europe, you can go directly to a pharmacist and request medication. You don't need a prescription from a doctor. Not only that, if I were to go to a doctor, I would need my mother's approval. I make a trip to the local pharmacist and scan the pharmacy to make sure I don't know anyone. I approach the counter with an air of confidence to hide the fact that I might not be—not in the face of this request. The pharmacist asks questions about my health, has me step on the scale, and prescribes birth control. It was as easy as that! He says that it's low-dose birth control, and if I have any problems with it, I should schedule an appointment with the doctor and titrate down. I think, *that's not happening*. Thankfully, I don't have any problems because I have no intention of sharing my sex life with my mom. I share many things with my mother, but conversations about anything sexual aren't encouraged. I'm sure my mother still thinks I believe her story about the birds and the bees and that the stork brought me home!

Being in a small school, I develop a close network of friends. Sometimes we go on fun day trips or weekend outings to other towns. Often, a classmate announces that we will meet in town at a local restaurant, at our favorite bar, or on the beach for a party. I rarely abuse alcohol, telling others I'm high on life. This is secretly a lie. Actually, I have control issues and don't want to let down my guard for fear of something happening to me. Plus, my mom tells me to watch over my sister, and I take my responsibility to heart. People crack jokes that my sister and I are joined at the hip. Her friends become my friends and my friends hers. I make rules that my date has to love, not like, my sister. I won't go out on a date without my sister. Sonya doesn't seem to mind being the third wheel. She isn't at an age where she's interested in dating, and we are so close that it doesn't seem odd to either of us. I'm sure it's strange for my date, but I don't worry if he thinks it's weird. It is non-negotiable.

My friends and I often meet after school at our favorite beach restaurant and squeeze some homework in. The open-aired restaurant has a thatched palm-leaf roof. There's a large bar in the center, and the restaurant cranks the best reggae music. A group of small tables and chairs encircles the bar. It always feels as if half the school is there. We prop our books on the bar and try to finish as much homework as we can before we hit the beach—which is not always easy when the sand and sea call us.

Kids start talking about going to Grenada in the Sierra Nevadas for a ski trip. I really miss skiing from my time in boarding school. The thought of getting up early to be one of the first people on the mountain sounds euphoric. Mom is very trusting about us traveling together because we are in a large group and look out for one another. When she agrees to let us go, I'm ecstatic.

When in a restaurant at the peak of the resort, I meet a guy named Danny from Madrid, who coincidentally happens to be a good friend of my old boyfriend, Robert, from boarding school. Because of this connection, I inherently trust him. Besides, he's extremely confident, well-spoken, extraverted, and gentlemanly.

"Hey, man, do you want to stop by and listen to my friend's band rehearse?" Danny asks. "They're super cool. I think you'll really like the rockin' tunes."

"Sure. Okay. Maybe. Where are they playing?" I ask.

"In our hotel room! We're staying at the Melia Sierra Nevada."

"Why not?"

"Cool. See you then." And he scurries off.

That night, I head to their room. I knock, but I doubt anyone can hear me over the blaring music. I test the doorknob, and it's not locked, so I let myself in. It's a cavernous room with an arched ceiling and six bunkbeds and a living room. The band jams in the middle beneath the arched ceiling. The Spanish rock and roll is so loud that the place pulsates, the guitars screech, and the lead singer screams at the top of his lungs. I see Danny across the room and wave. He seems happy to see me and waves me over. We try to talk, but it's nearly impossible until the band takes a break.

Danny introduces me to the band members. They seem cool but full of themselves and like they're looking for groupies. When Danny offers me a beer, I think *what the heck* and have two sips of it. We listen to the lead singer jam for a few songs, and that's the last thing I remember.

The next day, I wake up on the floor in the same place I had sat down when I entered the room the evening before. I'm all alone.

I'm so disoriented and can't believe I fell asleep there. My head feels heavy and dizzy. I'm nauseous, and I rub my face to snap out of my daze. I panic, realizing my friends are probably worried about where I am, so I want to get out of there quickly and let them know I'm okay. As I stand up, I notice my legs are like lead weights. I go to the bathroom to wash my face and pee and try to figure out why I feel so awful and why I'm sleeping on the floor. It's also 2:00 in the afternoon! I lost an entire day of skiing.

I notice my button up Levi jean pants are in complete disarray. Some of the buttons are mixed up and out of order. It is so odd because I am always careful to button-up my jeans properly. I like my T-shirts nicely tucked into my pants as well, and I realize my T-shirt is disheveled and untucked. When I sit on the toilet and began to pee, I feel an incredible burning sensation that takes my breath away. I hold onto the wall to manage the pain of peeing. *What the hell?! What happened to me?!* I know that I need to get out of there fast, and I'm worried my friends might be mad and upset since I didn't come home the night before.

When I cross the parking lot to my hotel, I see my friends walking through the parking lot with their skis headed into the direction of our hotel room. Stunned that I had overslept and lost a day of skiing, I call out for them. They look so relieved to see me and question me, but I have no memory of what had happened. I tell them that I fell asleep and just woke up. I feel terrible. I can see they are truly worried about me, and I'm grateful to be back with them.

Eduardo, my off-and-on boyfriend, currently off, is steaming and wants more details. I try to fill him in as much as possible, but it's difficult with no memory of the night before. As we were talking, the guys from the band happen to walk through the parking lot to get to their hotel. Eduardo quickly approaches them, and I assume he's asking them about last night. I can tell by their body language that something is off. Their eyes dart back and forth to look at me and then down at their shuffling feet. As the boys in the band walk away, they turn to look at me like something is wrong. When Eduardo rejoins me, he says it was a strange conversation and that they said I drank too much and crashed. I told him that it was impossible because I remember having only a few sips of a beer. He gives me a long look and recommends that I take a nap because I'm not looking so good. I sleep the entire day and wake up the next morning. I push it into the recesses of my memory as I hit the slopes and lose myself on the mountain, carving turns in the fresh powder, sometimes going too fast for my own good. But I don't care. I love the adrenaline rush of living on the edge of highspeed turns and catapulting down the mountain into a tree—a clump of a human taken by snow, ice, speed, and blunt force. Everyone would grieve a girl gone too soon, a girl so full of life. And only I would know my secret.

A week after my ski trip, I notice vaginal discharge in my underwear when I'm in the bathroom. *Strange. Did I have sex without knowing it? How could I not know? How did it happen? Did Danny and I have sex?* Date rape and being roofied aren't even in my vocabulary.

I want to tell my mom what happened, but I'm terrified of what she'll think of me and afraid she'll never allow me to go out again. I have no one to turn to.

The only person I can think to turn to is the pharmacist. I hurry over to the pharmacy and tell him what happened and describe my symptoms. He is so kind and advises me to see a doctor. He says it's a sexually transmitted disease called chlamydia, and he gives me an antibiotic to treat my symptoms. *What? How can I have a sexually transmitted disease when I didn't have sex? Chlamydia? Is that serious? Can I die from that?*

I want to ask the pharmacist but I'm too embarrassed, so I just walk out with a million questions whirling in my head.

I call Robert and tell him what happened with Danny. He exclaims, "What the hell?!" and says he's going to confront Danny. An hour later, he calls me back and says he asked Danny if he touched me. Danny's exact words were, "Oh, heck no. But things got a little crazy. You know how things get crazy sometimes."

He tells me he's done with Danny. Forever.

After the incident with Danny and his friends, my recurring nightmares intensify. In one dream, masked white faces press on top of me, one at a time, forcing me to have sex. The masks have open mouths and dark sockets for eyes, like in the movie *Scream*; they're someone and no one—vacant, sinister forces. No words come out of the gaping mouths, only slow, garbled, haunting noises. Each masked entity moves slowly on top of me, and then another white mask appears. Only my head and chest are visible; the rest of my body is absent.

Along with this nightmare, the fractured dreams torment me. The dreams are out of order, some repetitive, some fragments, like an unfinished puzzle. I keep feeling the need to piece the puzzle together, but so many pieces are missing. I go on a frantic search for the missing pieces and can't find them. If only I could finish the puzzle, the dreams would stop. My dad's face appears, then distorts like a spook in a haunted house. When I reach out to touch him to see if he's real, he disappears. Then he appears again as a phantom. Someone is fondling my privates; it feels wrong, but at times, it feels good. I'm disgusted. The dreams are so intense that they overtake my body and I wake up drenched in sweat. Whenever I feel like this, I'm compelled to plunge into the water to purify myself. When I swim in the pool, I stroke toward sunbeams and catch them with my hands—to touch the purifying light. As the water washes over me, I swim out the dirty, shameful feelings, the angst and emerge mentally and emotionally clean.

Are these memories instead of dreams? Did my dad force himself on me as a young girl? We couldn't have had sex because I bled like a virgin. *Did I bury the memories because they were so traumatic?*

I shove the thoughts out of my mind. They terrify me. The dreams linger throughout the day, and as much as I try, I can't shake them. Acting like a self-absorbed teenager and doing crazy things is the only way to distract me from the living hell. I follow my daredevil instinct and love scaring myself. I ski runs that I have no business skiing, and I swim in the ocean at night out past the breaker. I know it's dangerous but something about it is euphoric. I feel more alive when I'm flirting with death.

Once a full dream sequence occurs, I don't usually continue to have dreams about that incident; instead, a new sequence unfolds. When the sequences in my dreams return, and I can't ignore them, I keep track of them in a journal. I can't shake how real they feel. If I record my nightmare or memory or whatever it is, the pages hold the secrets instead of my mind, and I can close the book and walk away. I don't know what's happening to me, so I don't ask my parents if the dreams have seeds of truth. I don't want them to think I'm going crazy.

As I struggle with the fatigue of the incessant dreams, my dad returns to Spain from Saudi Arabia. When we greet him at the door, I muster all my willpower not to vomit when he embraces me. When he launches into his long-winded travel tales, I check out. Just seeing him relaxing and reading triggers unadulterated hatred. It deepens my sadness. I feel trapped by my revulsion. I feel disgusted about what happened and that it happened to me. I feel ugly inside and outside. The only way to stop the ugly is by ending it all.

I escape by sleeping more, even in the daytime. But sleep doesn't offer the escape I so desperately need. The nightmares torment me while I nap. Just being in my dad's presence and seeing him in dreams makes me feel that the dreams are, in fact, real memories.

CHAPTER 4
DREAMS AS MEMORIES

Out of the yearly 63,000 sexual abuse cases substantiated, or found strong evidence, by Child Protective Services (CPS),6 the perpetrator was most often the parent [1](rainn.org)

"So this was betrayal. It was like being left alone in the desert at dusk without water or warmth. It left your mouth dry and will broken. It sapped your tears and made you hollow."
-Anna Godbersen

I've stared at the ceiling for way too long, processing the fragments of my dreams. I've reread my journal with the reoccurring parts of my dream and the newer additions. My journal looks like a mad preschooler scribbled the newer portions. When I write, I close my eyes to envision what I saw in my dream. The streetlights cast immovable shadows. That's how I know he's coming; my dad's dark silhouette moves toward me, and he whispers. I loathe the sound of his whisper and the foul stench of his breath. I hate it so much. I jab the point of my pen into the paper of my journal just to feel a sense of release from the angry hate that bubbles up inside me.

I jab so hard that I create a hole—a hole where the light can shine through.

"Shhh, come with me." "Move over" "Shhh…" The many ways he beckons me flash through time and years. Intuitively, I know these words have been whispered so many times—his mouth so close, the words tickle my ears. The feeling of dread overtaking my mind and body. The feeling of wanting to scream. The knowing that Dad will hurt me or someone else if I don't obey him. The knowing that he owns me. The feeling of being helplessly too little. Nobody can see me or help me. The longing to be back in my warm bed, dreaming of little girl things like dolls, drawing, and playing with my friends.

I feel Dad's giant hand on my forearm as he pulls me up. His grip is firm but gentle enough, so I don't panic. I can see now that he intentionally creates a false sense of security so I will come along. He pretends to be lighthearted, but I'm too naive to see he's a fake. He's the chameleon I would catch as a girl. He's that mega black widow who spins his poisonous web like the one mom found in the corner coat closet. Yet, I can feel my desire to be respectful and be good. I want Dad to be happy so he won't hate me. I want to be loved.

Dad leads me down the pitch-black hallway, holding onto my hand, my body clammy with terror. The hallway opens to our living room, where the streetlight filters through the sheer curtains with flowers on them. What Dad does to my body…I can barely make out or recall much. My mind blocks so many of these memories to save me. I can see that now. It's okay that I don't remember so much of this part. It still doesn't make me feel less shame, less dirty, less angry, or disgust. It doesn't make all the rest untrue.

As I write down each repeating dream fragment in my journal, I piece together what my mind shows me from the past. Eventually, the shards form a whole memory. Once I have an intact memory, my mind reveals newer fragments of another memory and the exhausting process repeats. My mind shows me a film of my childhood but only in short takes, so I'm not overwhelmed by the feature film of my early years. I have so much love and respect for the way my mind has protected me, but at the same time, I hate my mind for revealing my past. I thought I had a normal childhood filled with swimming pools and Barbie dolls in the sun. Instead, a sinister monster has crawled out from the dusty bowels of my brain—a monster I call Dad.

But maybe he can't help it. He's damaged from his early childhood years during World War II. His memories are of constant hunger and vulnerability, once licking the back of the wallpaper for the dried flour glue to fill his aching belly. As trouble increased in the villages, my dad, who was in elementary school at the time, and his older brother were shuffled from family member to family member in different villages, as castaways of war.

I feel for him, but nothing excuses his behavior as an adult. I flip through my journal and see years of sexual abuse and physical abuse unraveling in these pages. It is me in the ink-and charcoal-smeared pages with drawings of occasional monsters. The monsters make me run for my life. Every bone in my body says these pages don't lie. *Well, do they?*

I'm back to staring at the ceiling as I lie on my bed with my hands behind my head. The cream-colored ceiling needs a fresh coat of paint, and there is a tiny dust bunny in the left corner of the ceiling. The light breeze from my bedroom window and the draft from the bedroom doorway makes the dust bunny on the web-like thing dance. The thought of a web brings my thoughts back to Dad and how he's been home for several weeks. The increase in nightmares. My adverse reaction to wanting to vomit when he greeted me with a hug—what was that all about? The lingering question of why Mom has not contacted a doctor about my ongoing nightmares. If I were a mom, I'd think my kid was sick and get medical help. Maybe I am sick. She's usually so attentive when it comes to our health. Why has she not questioned these things?

The dust bunny in the corner still quivers in the wind. A surge of energy blasts through my body as I sit up. No more staring at the ceiling, wondering if these things really happened to me. I'm going to confront him. My face burns, my heart beats in my throat, and I break out in a clammy sweat. Instead of confronting Dad, I want to run past him out the door and never return. I never return to a father who's a midnight predator and a mother who's a daytime coward. Sonya is just an innocent bystander, but I'm annoyed with her, too. The people you trust the most with your life are the ones who violate and betray you. I'm shaking with rage and anxiety. What if he denies it? Then I'll question whether it really happened. *Am I really doing this?* The cool marble floor under my bare feet reminds me that this is real, and, yes, I am doing this. I'm going to figure this all out right now.

Dad sits at the dining room table, his newspaper obscuring most of his face. He peers out from the page of his paper and says, "Hey, Cindy baby. What's going on?"

I have my arms crossed over my chest in a standoff pose, and I'm peering down at him. I'm going for bluster, but inside I feel fragile. I hope he doesn't notice. "So, Dad, I've been having these dreams for months and months now. Well, they are really nightmares and well... did you touch me when I was little?" I blurt without finesse.

Dad sets down his paper and glares at me with his round intense, blue eyes. His mouth forms a smile, and he laughs. He shifts in his seat from side to side, giggling, and says, "Well what have you been reading?"

I nervously glance away. I wasn't expecting him to laugh at me. What did I think he would say? *Why, yes Cindy, I molested you. Terribly sorry about that. Where should we have dinner tonight?* A criminal never admits to their crime when asked point blank. I knew this! They live in denial that they are even a criminal because they justify their actions. What an idiot I am! Now I'm pissed that I heard his response and pissed off at myself for my stupidity. Did I think an apology could instantly erase the past like a magic wand?! *Thanks, Dad, now I feel so much better knowing the truth.* I spent so much time thinking about this moment, anticipating the confrontation, the moment of truth, and maybe hoping for regret and redemption. I never thought this part through—not rationally, at least. Can I help it if my heart yearns for an apology? Can I help it if I want to save my childhood with a redemptive father? Can I help it if I want him to be someone he's not?

Dad has several newspapers fanned out in front of him—*The New York Times*, *The Wall Street Journal*, and the local newspaper written in Spanish. He has circled a few household items and a paragraph. *Why did he do that?* He doesn't even read Spanish. He gets by with survival Spanglish, so maybe he can read Spanish well enough. I take a vacation in my head after my Dad's response. My finger circles the highlighted outline of the article, again and again. I'm lost in the circle, the newsprint, the Spanish words. Then I snap back to reality.

"You don't remember anything like that?" I finally say, searching his face for the apology I so desperately need to stay sane and alive.

"No, girl," he says, pitifully shaking his head. His bizarre, exaggerated grin is gone and replaced by a look of concern like I had lost my marbles. "Why would you say such a thing? You know I love you so much and don't know why you would want to hurt me like that," he says, his voice halting.

I feel a flick of guilt but remind myself it's me, not him who suffered. "But, Dad, I'm retrieving memories of what happened to me," I say in a high-pitched whine because it's obvious he doesn't believe me. Feeling on the defensive and deflated, my eyes brim with tears. My hands tremble from the rush of adrenaline, fearing what might happen next. I picture myself writing for months to save myself—painstakingly knitting the memories back together. Those months felt like a year, like half a lifetime. I urge myself not to cry and try to focus on his words. I hold back a rush of tears, afraid that if I don't, I might never stop crying.

"So where did your memories go?" Dad says with a sarcastic shrug. "You dreamt about this? What does that mean?" He chuckles in amusement, then becomes serious again. He leans across the table and affectionately taps my arm. "You know what I think? I think you read this somewhere or you saw it in a movie. Oh, Cindy, did something happen to you?" He says with moist eyes.

With that performance, a four-alarm bell goes off in my head. I can sense a lie in his piercing blue eyes—as if his intense gaze will convince me that I fabricated this story. I glare at him in silence. *This psycho gets an Academy Award for his performance! Too good to be true, Dad.* I knew in my gut that my horrific dreams were real memories. I'm not sure why I forgot such terrible things or why they were flooding back now, but I knew he was lying. He couldn't disguise his lies with words, tears, or affectionate gestures. I had caught him off guard, and he played every part of his lie perfectly by belittling me, turning things around, producing tears from supposed disappointment over my accusations. *I see you, Dad. I see your stinking lie!* I confidently shake my head. He told me all I needed to know.

He jumps up from the table, agitated, and races to tell Mom about our discussion before I do. It's another clue that he's lying. Guilty players often play immediate offense and bend the ears of others to convince them first that their words are the truth. I stay back to see Mom's reaction. I suppose I could have scurried over to her first, but that's not my style. I like to wait and see how things unfold. I can see the character of a person much more clearly by their reactions or lack of actions. I'm not very trusting. I've noticed if I react quickly, I get caught up in the drama. I miss the reality of the situation and can't see the person's true nature or intentions.

I've known bullies like my Dad on the playground. They cry out the loudest when they have their back against the wall. The bully convinces others that their reality is the only one. They generally have sway, popularity, or status. The bully makes loudmouth comments about others with humor or pain and gains popularity. Even as a kid, I could pick out the adult bullies.

People flock to them like moths to light. I call these followers "the sheep." Sadly, I had to accept that Mom's a sheep. The sheep seek comfort by going with the flow. They fear being cast out of the group, not being popular, or disturbing their comfort zone. They say things such as "That's not my business" or "This is not my fight" to justify not helping the person being picked on. They turn on family members or close friends to keep the peace. The bully is emboldened by their loyalty and gains more power. Deep down inside, the bully is broken, truly unhappy, and very insecure. Dad has a wardrobe of many masks he wears for mom, and she falls for his manipulation. It sucks for me!

Mom scurries toward me at the kitchen table. "You know how hard your father works to provide us with such a beautiful lifestyle. He makes such sacrifices for us to live like this!"

If I were normal, I would have dropped to my knees and balled upon hearing Mom's words. I saw her truth too. She's a big fat liar like Dad. I'm deep in thought, so I tune out part of her rant. I hear, "You are causing trouble in the household," and then I blank out again. "Now, please apologize to your father for hurting his feelings."

I watch as her big eyes squint in pain and her giant mouth moves up and down like a Muppet. With disgust I think, *Really? You're such a coward, Mom.*

Mom's a sheep who goes along with the bully for fear of stirring the pot. It looks like Mama doesn't want to rock the boat over this one. *I'm worth the fight over your lifestyle, Mom. How did you become so spineless? Your love is so confusing!*

I generally stand up for what I believe even if it makes me an outsider. I'd rather be true to my beliefs than be a sheep. *What a lie of a life! Mom, can't you see you're compromising your nature out of fear?*

I meekly apologize to dad and receive a group hug that I don't even feel. I'm so steeled against them and their lies. This ending is neat and tidy for my parents, but I hate them both.

My parents want me to doubt myself. Should I pretend that none of this happened? How do I endure this? How can I live with a monster in the house?

I can barely lift my feet up to climb the few stairs to my bedroom. Defeated and fatigued, I close my bedroom door and plop face down on my bed.

Sonya asks, "What's going on out there?"

"Apparently, it was nothing. I'm nothing. I hate those guys!" I cry into my pillow. I don't want them to hear me. I felt weak, like they have won something— piece of my soul, a piece of my heart, a piece that I wonder if I can ever retrieve.

Sonya sits cross-legged on her bed. "What's wrong?" But I have no energy to share. She asks again, "What happened?"

"It's nothing. Alright?!"

"Fine. Then shut up!" She says and chucks a pillow at my head. "It must be one of those dreams."

"Shut up!" I giggle at her silliness and cry at the same time. Inside, I ache like a giant bleeding ulcer.

After Dad leaves for Saudi Arabia again, Mom invites me to sleep in her room so she can reach out and comfort me back to sleep. It's odd for a seventeen-year-old, but I find so much comfort in knowing that she's there and I'm safe.

Every time Dad returns, repressed memories resurface in my dreams. The sound of his voice and his presence trigger so much anger in me that I leave the room and journal furiously to release the rage from my body. I go for a run after journaling and journal again when I return home. I have a thick pad of lined paper and vigorously write to the point where the words are almost illegible.

Then I wad up the seething words and throw them on the floor—little hate bombs. When I release all my hate onto pieces of paper, I calm myself and look at the pile of scrunched-up paper around me. Sometimes I save a few notes and read them later. With disgust, rage, and shame, I slip into a depression. I completely avoid my dad as my childhood memories return, one at a time.

They're dreams of me running for my life, screaming, "No! No! No!" My sister wakes me up in the middle of the night. "It's just a nightmare, Cindy. Everything's okay. Go back to sleep."

But the haunting dreams continue, and Sonya copes with it by hurling her pillow at my head.

My dreams start to shift dramatically, and I find my voice, saying everything I wanted to say to my dad as a child but never could. I hear the clinking of a glass in my bedroom, smell the alcohol, and someone's dark presence over my bed. I have the desire to kill, and the words "I hate you!" burst forth from me. I scream, "Noooooo!" and wake myself up. I wake up exhausted from fighting back, filled with incredible shame and fatigue. The shame hangs over me like a wet blanket. It is a different form of entrapment than I have ever experienced before.

I'm so wrung out and depressed from reliving my past. Being with friends makes me feel worse. I don't have the emotional bandwidth to have fun or laugh about silly teenage things. When they are being light and funny, it's hard for me. It takes more emotion to fake it than to be myself. I feel like a farce. I'm incognito, an imposter dressing up as me. Meeting outside or listening to music is okay, but I can't stand parties, so slowly, I withdraw from my friends.

The only things that bring me comfort are journaling and being outside. I cope through exercise and devote a lot of time to journaling. I write down any thought that comes to mind and throw it away immediately. This action creates the feeling that I'm in control of getting rid of a memory the way I want to. I try reading the written memory, but it often only further depresses me, so I write it down, rip it up, and throw it away. I shred the memories into the tiniest pieces—which is much more gratifying than just throwing it away. I know I have a lot of hate for my dad, but it becomes apparent to me that I harbor more self-loathing.

To shake the heavy cloud I live with, I take long barefoot walks on the beach, trying to appreciate the beauty of the water. Sometimes I can't, so I just focus on the beauty of the color blue. I notice the warmth of the sun on my face. I focus on the sensation of the sand under my feet and between my toes. I often feel nothing inside, but the cool air from the water and the other natural elements makes me feel something. I relish running barefoot in the soft sand and letting my mind wander. Every morning, I do one hundred sit-ups, helping me to clear out the cobwebs in my head and get me going. Exercise becomes a way of life to help with de-stressing from school. It also helps shave off a few extra pounds.

I seek inspiration from books and discover Edgar Allen Poe's writing—chockful of dread and misery. I love this stuff! His life is shittier than mine. I realize other people are hurting too. I didn't know that everyone goes through pain. Why? Because everyone seems happy. I read and reread his poem for comfort. His words from so long ago leap from the page and hold my brokenness. His words do what no one in my family can do—help me see that I am not alone.

Alone

From childhood's hour I have not been
As others were; I have not seen
As others saw; I could not bring
My passions from a common spring.
From the same source I have not taken
My sorrow; I could not awaken
My heart to joy at the same tone;
And all I loved, I loved alone,
Then- in my childhood, in the dawn
Of a most stormy life- was drawn
From every depth of good and ill
The mystery which binds me still:
From the torrent, or the fountain,
From the red cliff of the mountain,
From the sun that round me rolled
In its autumn tint of gold,
From the lightning in the sky
As it passed me flying by,
From the thunder and the storm,
And the cloud that took the form,
(When the rest of Heaven was blue)
Of a demon in my view.

In my darkest days, I'm out of control, and it scares me. When I peer at my reflection in the mirror, styling my thick hair, I see a demon looking back at me—an exhausted demon. I feel so dirty and ugly.

Why are my cheeks so puffy? I look like a human blowfish. I hate that about myself! I suck in my cheeks, but that isn't any better. *And why are my lips so big?* I bite my lips so now I'm lipless. *That's even worse!* I release them and they puff up again. *Why am I so skinny with such hairy arms? I look like an anorexic ape!*

But then a strange thing happens. I laugh out loud at the words "anorexic ape." My laughter breaks the spell of me digging my early grave. I think, *Stop it, Cindy! Just stop it! There must be something you like about yourself. One thing. Find just one thing.* I search my face for one thing. Anything. *I love my eyebrows. I love my eyebrows.* Then I say it aloud, "I love my eyebrows." I say it again, "I love my eyebrows." They frame my eyes like parentheses, directing my gaze back to my eyes absorbing pain, light, and beauty. I'm grateful to my eyes for seeing—really seeing. Not just perceiving what I'm supposed to like an obedient foot soldier.

Every day begins like this—challenging myself to find something. Anything that I like. Each time I read the notes, I repeat the words, sometimes twenty times. If a negative thought arises, I peer into the mirror and say it again and again until I feel something. Even if I only feel anger or boredom—it is something. I know I'm alive and feeling. Sometimes, I truly feel the words, and I am gratified in feeling good.

The first mantra I write is: *I love myself. I love myself. I love you.* Sometimes I say my name, and it intensifies the mantra. What I don't realize at the time is that these are my first steps toward self-healing; the more I write, whether mantras or memories, the more I walk through the pain.

I go from a place of almost losing myself to fighting to be whole again. I had a tenacious spirit as a girl, repeating the refrain, *Dad's not going to win.* I remind myself that he didn't take anything from me, and he won't win. When my suicidal thoughts lure me to the edge, I remember how water saved me. I return to the coping strategies I used as a kid help me through the dark days.

I had a ritual after Dad molested me. It started when I watched my neighbor, Maria, as she was baptized in a swimming pool. I asked her if she felt different afterward. She said, "No, but I feel cleaner."

When I couldn't shake the storm that had settled in my mind, I jumped into the neighbor's swimming pool, and the world became hushed, buoyant, cleansing. I stayed submerged until the water absorbed the impurities, lightened my burden, and purified me.

If I couldn't swim, I'd jump into the shower and watch the water rinse off the shame for the things my father had done to me. It felt good to wash the filth from his fingerprints down the drain. I'm not exactly sure when this ritual started, but I was still sculpting silly creatures out of Play-Doh, fingerpainting, and skittering over jungle gyms with my friends.

At 17, my toes grip the edge of the swimming pool, and I gaze down at my rippled reflection. I dive into my image, shattering my thoughts and view of myself. As I sink to the bottom, each inch of water rinses off more dirty feelings from being touched by greedy, depraved hands in my childhood bed, a sacred place intended for sweet dreams. I see my bed filled with dolls, including some that cry, "Mama," so my mom will awaken and come to my rescue. I push my butt out so there's no room for interlopers in my bed. I surface, propel myself out of the pool and, once again, stand at the water's edge. I pray for this dive to wash all the filth from my dad's grubby hands taking what wasn't his: Innocence. Trust. Purity. Goodness. Diving into the pool to cleanse my heart makes me better afterward. I am pure, as if he had never tainted my body.

I hold my breath and try to reach the other end of the pool in one breath. Sometimes I make it to the end, but what matters most is the feeling that my mind and body are clean and that whatever happened at my house is erased.

The sun's rays dance on the ripples and illuminate the ones from my strokes. The reflected light creates soft hexagon shapes dancing on the bottom of the pool—so magical! I stretch my arms out with all my might to reach the next ripple in front of me. I reach the other side of the pool and stand with my back against the sun, gazing at my shadow on the bottom of the pool. I wave my arms around and track myself in the shadow. I look like an angel. I like the thought of that. It's comforting.

Sometimes I sit on the shower's tile floor. I turn on the warm water, and the showerhead sprays on top of my head.

Today at school, the word "stupid" owned me. I felt incompetent in every class. "Ugly" because that's what I see in the mirror and feel inside. "Dirty" because my nightmares fill me with shame.

I visualize each word in large black letters washing away. The dark, bold words slide down my body and into the drain. As they disappear, I tell myself that the words have no power over me. But I know that by next week, they will attempt a comeback, and I'll have to do it all over again. I wonder if I'll ever be free from their stranglehold.

Sometimes I write the words with my favorite felt pens on a piece of paper and bring the paper into the shower. I like to watch the words wash off the paper under the water's spray.

One time, Mom catches me. She opens the bathroom door. "What in God's name are you doing taking a shower with a piece of paper? That's weird, Cindy. You've been in there for 20 minutes. You're running up our gas bill," Mom scolds.

"We don't pay for gas. It's included in our rent," I say dryly, wondering why she's barging into my shower.

"Don't forget who you are talking to, young lady. You know I would never talk to my mother that way." She closes the door.

I don't care. She doesn't know what it's like to live with the stain of abuse. Water cleanses my heart and saves me from desolation.

As the dreary days of winter brighten and warm, I feel less burdened by my thoughts and memories, and I venture out more with friends. I find myself drawn to laughter; a great belly laugh is healing and restorative. Sometimes I dance and sing myself silly with my sister to lighten my feelings. We dance until we're dripping with sweat or a neighbor knocks on the door and says, "Por favor, bajen la música!" (Turn down the music.) Usually, it's writing or moving my body that creates a shift away from the heaviness I carry inside my head and heart. With each passing summer day, I feel more equipped with tools to combat the hard days. With friends and family who stay by my side, the thick fog of depression begins to lift.

Yet so many questions remain.

CHAPTER 5
STATESIDE

"The truth will set you free. But first, it will piss you off."
-Gloria Steinem

L iving overseas has opened my eyes; it has helped me view the US from an outsider's perspective. When you're a child living overseas, you learn that what we do in the US impacts people around the world. Even European children are up on current affairs in the US. Understanding our country's influence in the world makes me proud to be an American.

I miss the silly things I took for granted when living in the US, such as Disneyland, Hollywood, and the beauty of the Grand Canyon. I've become more politically aware, and I appreciate the freedom to express my religious and political opinions and the abundant opportunities in the US. This growing social awareness makes me value being an American even more. I admire the happy, ambitious, driven nature of Americans. I've become very patriotic and yearn to be home.

There's just one problem. I'm the only one in my family who feels this way. As my high school graduation nears, my mom and dad discuss the possibility of living in Europe permanently. Sonya likes the idea, too.

Every cell in my body resists the notion. "I need to go home and grow roots," I say.

"You're too young to grow roots!" My mom says.

When my parents say I'm outnumbered and we are staying, I say, "Be my guest, but I want an American college experience." Not only am I homesick, but I also want to finish my final months of high school in the States. I have the most ridiculous list of why I want to return, but it makes all the difference to me:

1. I want to eat a hamburger in a restaurant with dill pickles and a yummy secret sauce.

2. I want to date an American boy—one who plays baseball and football. (Our family isn't into sports, so my parents think I'm crazy.)

3. I want wall-to-wall carpeting. All the homes we've lived in overseas have had marble floors with throw rugs.

My laundry list of all the things I miss goes on and on. The more I think about them, the more I realize the extent of my homesickness. I'm determined to go back to the States—with or without my family. My burgeoning independence scares my mom. She says she can't live without either of her daughters. With my dad's absence in Spain, the three of us have become very close.

Although Mom isn't happy about it, my parents agree to move back to the US. My dad chooses the Northwest because when he first came to the US via Vancouver, Canada, he was struck by the region's beauty.

Shortly after deciding to return, my dad lands an engineering job in Tacoma, Washington, an urban port city 30 miles southwest of Seattle. As excited as I am to go home, it is a huge culture shock. I go from bikinis on the beach to down coats in the drizzle. I've never experienced anything like Tacoma's rain, which can drag on for weeks. I'd also grown accustomed to cozy living quarters. In our new home, we are so spread out; I feel disconnected from Sonya and Mom. I'm often in a state of "grumpy cakes," as my mom calls it. It makes me laugh when she says it.

I struggle to assimilate to my own culture. With my slight British accent picked up from attending overseas schools, I say things like, "That's brilliant!" instead of "That sounds great!" or "Where's the loo? I need to wash up!" instead of "Where's the bathroom? I need to wash my hands." When my classmates laugh at me, I crack up. It's amusing to sound like a foreigner in my own country.

Adding to my culture shock, we return partway through my senior year, and the social activities in American high schools feel foreign to me. I'm shocked by the segregated groups of jocks, stoners, cheerleaders, nerds, and miscellaneous cliques. In European schools, kids didn't form separate groups based on interests or associations; we were just individuals. Because I socialized with all kinds of kids in Europe, I fit into many different groups. I really can't be pigeonholed, even though I resonate the most with the nerds.

I'm also surprised that religion shapes social life with its after-school programs and activities. In Europe, religion didn't factor into people's everyday lives—only during holidays. I am asked to Tolo, a girl-picks-boy-dance, and Homecoming, and I've never heard of either of those dances. Some friends attend the Apple Cup (the big game between Washington State University and the University of Washington), and I think it's an event centered around apple-eating! I haven't been to an indoor mall in years—such an anomaly to shop in one easy location. I marvel at the well-maintained roads and not having to watch my footing on sidewalks. I'm used to looking out for potholes and broken-up sidewalks; I had grown accustomed to looking down instead of up.

I take joy in the things I missed while living overseas. I don't understand the rules of football or baseball, but I love attending games with friends, and cheering at the top of our lungs. I indulge in hamburgers and hotdogs and live out what I had imagined American teenage life to be. Our home has wall-to-wall carpeting, and I love lying on the shag carpet, moving my arms back and forth as if making a snow angel. No more cold marble floors.

My classmates are planning for college and their careers; people seem laser-focused on what's next. I like the driven vibe, but it is worlds away from the laid-back feeling of beach life in Torremolinos. I'm intrigued by the way music, TV shows, and movies are an intricate part of American life that dictates trends and fashion. People constantly discuss shows like *Dynasty*, *General Hospital,* and *Beverly Hills 90210*. If I watched TV overseas, it was in a different language, so I focused on reading subtitles and rarely got attached to shows.

Sharing a house with my dad is a huge adjustment. I wasn't used to being in his space. I haven't spent consistent time since I was 13. I didn't avoid him. I thought he was a weirdo, and I didn't listen to him babble, but I was moving toward acceptance. I indulged in being a teen.

Thankfully, he works a lot, including overtime, so we don't see each other very often. He feels like a stranger to me, but when he's around, he seems happy we're together.

In contrast, my mom isn't happy being back in the States, mostly because she's around my dad too much. She had grown accustomed to his traveling for work, and the transition to him being home every night is difficult. She naps a lot and withdraws from conversations. I know how much she loved life in Spain, and I feel guilty for wanting to come back. Mom frequently visits her family. She says it's too expensive for them to visit and easier for her to travel to their homes. The truth is that she's embarrassed by my dad's strange behavior and the sad state of their relationship.

"I don't want my family knowing about your father and asking too many questions. Please don't mention anything that goes on in our household," she says.

If we had had more family around over the years, they would have seen my dad's erratic behavior and my mom's fear of him and addressed it with her. In the beginning, my grandmother wasn't supportive of my mom leaving my dad, but later, when she realized he was unhealthy for her, she encouraged Mom to leave.

Although there's an extra bedroom in our home, I refuse to sleep alone; instead, I bunk with Sonya, who brings me comfort. I've never slept in my own bedroom, and I don't want to start now. Despite things going well, my nightmares persist with the recurring theme of being trapped or stuck. I shout, "No!" With my mouth barely open, distorted sounds escape. I try to say, "Stop," but the word is muffled, and I wake up, restless and sweating. Like in Spain, my sister hurls a pillow at my head to get me to wake from my nightmares. As the dreams progress, I shout, "Dad, I hate you! Stop!"

She never questions it, but she jokes and says, "You're having another hateful dream towards Dad!" and laughs. Although I don't interact much with my dad, my past still stalks me.

I decide to attend the local community college, so I can be near Mom. Sonya graduates a year early from high school, attends a local university, and decides to live at home. Mom needs a go-between to deal with Dad, so Sonya and I fulfill that role. I work a part-time job, and after my classes, I spend time with my boyfriend and friends. I often travel on the weekends to go skiing, hiking, and sailing. Sonya's more suited for home life than me. She loves my dad's intellectual side and engages in conversations about politics and current events.

I save money to travel but keep in mind that Mom's afraid she won't be able to support herself if she leaves. I want to help her in any way I can.

My sister and I try simple things to make my mom smile. She loves swings, and whenever we come across a swing set, we stop for a little playtime. We throw our heads back and laugh as we swing carefree like children. For a moment, it seems she forgets she's trapped in a loveless marriage. Despite these happy times, all the laughter in the world can't change her situation. Even though she returns to work as a bank teller, which I thought might cheer her up, she doesn't attempt to hide her misery.

One day, I decide to have a heart-to-heart talk with her. I've been thinking a lot about Mom. Who is she, really? Does she not see what is happening to her? Why is she so paralyzed?

She and I are on swings in a nearby playground. We had just competed to see who can swing to the highest point, and I let her win. But we don't want to leave the swings, not yet. We're grasping the chain-links and swinging slowly toward stillness, dragging our feet in the dirt.

"Mom?"

"Yes, sweetie?"

"You know you're my best friend, right?"

"Oh, I am? That's so sweet, Cindy."

"Why would someone betray their best friend?"

She sighs, gazing down at her feet. "I'm only human. We're all fallible."

"I don't get you, Mom."

"I don't get you at all most of the time."

We laugh with so much respect and love for each other.

"You're so weird. How did I get such a weird kid?"

"I love you more."

"I love you more," she says.

"Mom…"

"Yes, honey?"

"Why don't you just leave him?"

She turns to look at me. "Oh, honey. It's not as easy as that. Where will I go? How will I make a decent living? Who will pay for your college?"

"We'll figure it out. Don't worry about our college. Your happiness is more important than anything."

"I can't leave you girls."

"I would rather have you be healthy and happy."

"Your dad provides a comfortable life for us."

"Who cares about material things if you're unhappy?" I don't understand why material things matter so much that she's willing to be miserable.

For a minute, she looks vulnerable, as if she might admit her life is killing her and will do something about it. But she straightens her posture, jumps up from the swing, brushes off her pants, and says, "No, Cindy. We have a good life. Many people don't. We should be thankful and make the best of it."

I clench my jaw, trying to contain my disappointment. It upsets me that she's choosing to stay with Dad and make herself a martyr.

Sonya and I encourage her to move out with us, to start a new life, but she refuses, so we feel obligated to stay home to protect her. She is depressed, emotionally trapped, and struggling in her loveless relationship. If I leave, that will create more drama, and my sister will take the emotional brunt, which I cannot bear. Leaving the house isn't an option for Sonya or my mother. I feel too much love for them to walk away. I've always felt compelled to protect my mother and sister, even as I was being abused as a child.

On a weekday night when I was seven and Sonya five, we were doing our homework, and my mom periodically checked in on our assignments. My dad walked into the room while my mom folded clothes in another room, so I asked him for help on a math problem. He looked at the problem and then stared at me in disbelief. He threaded his fingers through my hair, so there wasn't even an inch to move, and with his other hand, he pressed firmly in between my shoulder blades to prevent me from moving. Then he slammed my head on the desk. He whipped my head up and down, screaming at the top of his lungs, "You are so stupid! How could you not understand this!"

As my head hit the table, I peered over at Sonya, who was sitting at her desk next to me. Our eyes locked, and hers grew enormous. She stood up, knocking over her desk. As the desk slammed into the floor, she screamed, "Mom!" She stood there frozen and crying, her face filled with terror. My dad continued screaming and slamming my head against the desk over and over again.

My mom darted in with her slippers, her neatly pressed skirt and apron, and her hair in its usual perfect updo. She ran to my side and put her hands underneath my face to shield my head from hitting the desk. She shouted at my dad and asked what he was doing. Before he could answer, she swatted at him to stop. He finally shouted back that he was trying to knock some sense into me and that we needed to focus harder and learn more. He accused my mom of not teaching us anything and chastised us for hiding under her coattails.

When my dad finally let go, I ran to Sonya and wrapped my arms around her. She still couldn't move and just stood there as I clung onto her. My dad stormed out of the room, and my mom rushed to inspect my head. She told me with teary eyes that I had a goose egg. Through my tears, I tried to convince my mom that I was okay, but Sonya was not. She was frozen in terror. My mom and I stood on either side of her and helped her walk to the corner of the room. The three of us huddled together and cried. My mom kept checking my head, and I told her to focus on Sonya.

Sonya didn't talk for days. She'd whisper a few things to Mom, but I became her voice. Sonya was much more sensitive than me, and I worried about her. Even at the dinner table, our mom would ask her if she wanted more food or milk, and I answered for her. Eventually, Dad noticed Sonya's silence and threatened to spank her if she didn't start talking. She ran to the bedroom in tears but resumed speaking right after this threat. She was terrified of him. And I thought, *I need to protect my mom and sister.*

Flooded with memories and filled with frustration, I think back on the events that led to us going to a shelter, the time we came close to escaping from Dad, the time my mom might've started a whole new life without the oppressive force of a man who didn't know how to love her, a man who preyed on her child. My mom might've found happiness had she been willing to risk living without him.

At eight, I snuck into my dad's office in our Arizona home and shook from the thought of being caught. I quickly rifled through the shoebox on the bottom of the office closet underneath more boxes. He had moved his boxes there after I had found them the last time. Whenever my parents left the house, I would go through their things, so I knew exactly where he had moved the inappropriate sexy photos of me.

In my mind, I had rehearsed this conversation so many times. I held onto one of the photos for the day and waited until the timing was right. My sister was out of the room, and my dad was at work.

Ironically, I felt that I was in the safest part of my house, my bedroom. I was playing on the carpet with my Barbies when my mom stopped at the doorway to check on me. I stared at her, and she stared right back. "Cindy, what's going on. Are you okay?"

I reached out my hand to my mother to motion for her to sit down with me. Her brows were furrowed, and I could see the deep stress line between. She kneeled and then sat on her ankles. Her legs were perfectly folded in half, and her bottom rested on her feet. I struggled to find the right words.

It was as if I had an ugly steel pit deep in the bottom of my stomach that held my voice. I desperately tried to move it up and out of my mouth. I opened my mouth, yet nothing would come out. It was as if my voice box were frozen. I could feel the pit making its way up. Mom's face contorted with concern. I looked down and focused on her beautiful tan legs and the hem of her dress as I stuttered. "D…D…Daddy t..t…touches me at night sometimes."

She stroked my hair and scooted closer while blinking. "What do you mean, he touches you?" Her eyes were full of fear as she tried to understand. I handed her the photo that I hid under my leg, sweating from sitting on it for hours.

She glanced at it and didn't say anything. She just reached out, pulled me in tightly, and cried. Our tears flowed and flowed, but no words were spoken. We didn't need words. She held me, we cried, and my tears soaked her shirt. The more we cried, the more the weight I didn't even know I had been carrying lifted. Despite feeling relieved that I'd told her, I couldn't shake the fear of what was going to come next. I worried my mom and sister would get hurt. I knew there would be trouble. I knew our world was going to change. She brushed my hair off my forehead and didn't release her embrace until I pulled away.

A month after I told Mom that my dad was touching me, she told the neighbors she was leaving my dad and taking my sister and me. No one liked him, so they were supportive.

Sonya and I were excited because she said we were going on vacation.

"Girls, pack your bags. I have some surprises planned for our trip, including a cute vacation home."

I was anxious to see our vacation home. When we pulled up to a house and parked along the street, I asked my mom where we were. She said Nogales, Arizona. It didn't seem like a vacation place. The houses were freshly painted with front yards smaller than my bedroom. They were bordered with short chain-link fences that you could step over. Kids played outside on the narrow street lined with row houses. They were tiny, but cozy.

An elderly couple greeted us in Spanish. She introduced them as our "other grandparents." They weren't our blood relatives, but they had a special place in our family. This elderly couple became my Abuelita and Abuelo. Abuelita only spoke Spanish and Abuelo spoke mainly Spanish and a little English. Their eyes were warm, and their embraces were wonderful. It wasn't until much later in life that I realized Abuelita and Abuelo were hosts of a shelter.

My mom never said anything about going home, so I wondered if we would stay in Nogales. For two and a half months, she kept up her story that we were on vacation, and in many ways, it felt like one. I was relaxed and felt a level of security that I didn't realize I lacked. Seeing my mom so happy, laughing loudly, so full of life was the best part of our time away. Before that, I couldn't remember Mom being happy. I wanted our vacation to last forever.

One evening after coming in for dinner, she called my sister and me to her room. "We have to go home."

I stared at her in disbelief. "Why can't you leave him for good?" My greatest fear had come true. We had come all this way only to have to return. At the shelter, she had support and help. I thought we were finally going to get some help, finally forging a new life, a new healthy family.

Mom said, "I worked it out with Dad. He won't touch you ever again." She assured me that things would be different. "Besides, this is a trial period. Anyways, if I leave your father, how would I meet anyone else?"

Something broke inside me that day. Any trust I placed in my mom had vanished. I thought, *You're not being a good mommy. If you're not going to protect me, I can only count on myself.*

I returned home a changed person. Instead of finding peace away from the monster, I was full of rage. Instead of finding safety, I was fighting for survival inside our home. I thought, *I might have to kill my dad to make it stop.* I went to bed every night with a knife (a butter knife because I didn't want to gouge myself) and practiced stabbing my pillow. When I eventually fell asleep, the knives clanked underneath my bed in a pile of protective cutlery. My mother discovered my stash and said, "Oh, here's all my cutlery!" But she never questioned why I might be sleeping with knives.

I hated who I was becoming—someone evil I didn't recognize. But I was at the breaking point, escalating out of control. If my dad tried to hit me, I'd punch or slap him. If he screamed at my mom or sister, I'd take cheap shots and clobber him from behind, or I'd side-kick him, sometimes in the balls. *Make it count*, I told myself. *Always make it count*. I sprinted away and wore my hair in a French braid so he couldn't grab my pigtails.

That's when my body fell apart with pink eye, ear infections, and repetitive tonsillitis, stomach problems, and diarrhea. I was fighting for my life.

One day, while Mom and I prepare chicken enchiladas in our kitchen in Tacoma, a burning question about our leaving the shelter arises. I want to ask Mom why she compromised herself, Sonya, and me by returning to Dad. I know it will hurt, but I've always wondered.

"Mom, why did you return to Dad after we went to the shelter?"

"To protect us."

You felt staying with Dad protected us?! The thought saddens and angers me. "I was anything but protected. If I had been you, I would've slept in the streets instead of returning home after learning the truth about Dad."

"I'm not you. I'm me."

It underscores our differences. I've learned if you surrender to passivity, you remain a victim. Because I was a victim so early, I know inaction is never the answer—at least not for me.

If Mom won't leave Dad without resources, maybe transitioning to a shelter will encourage her to leave. I research local shelters and programs that offer a new start. When I present my findings, she admits she can never leave. She says my suggestions are my steps that she must take her own. I'm disappointed but accept that she is doing her best. She fears the unknown and is too afraid to live on her own, compromising her values for the familiar. She feels she can live in both worlds and live a lie, pretending that we have a normal life.

With my memories flooding back, I have so many questions about my childhood. *Did I do something to make my dad sexually attracted to me? Had I dressed provocatively? Was I flirtatious? Or was I just a bad person who deserved it? Could I have fought harder?* Then my thoughts turn dark. *What would have happened if I had killed my dad? Am I a horrible person for even thinking that?* With the persistent and disturbing questions, I wonder if I should talk to someone about the abuse. Journaling and exercise help, but the only way I'll fully heal is by talking to a professional. However, I worry if I do, the therapist will be required by law to report the abuse. *Will my dad be charged, leaving my mom without a home and the things she values?*

I realize my hopes and dreams for my mom are fruitless. I can't live her life any more than she can live mine. As painful as it is, I must let go. It's my turn, and I can do things differently. I *will* do things differently. I'll start by emotionally separating from my family.

One morning over coffee, I say, "Mom, I've decided to start living for myself."

"Oh, really? What does that mean?" she says, pouring cream into her coffee.

"Well, to begin with, I'm not going to make dinner every night like I have since high school. I don't know who will, but it's not going to be me."

"My goodness, Cindy. What's gotten into you?"

I don't have an answer for that other than it is time to live my life. "Also, I can't be around Dad when he gets off work, and I'm done being a go-between. You guys will have to sort things out yourself."

"Aren't we being selfish?"

"You're the one who's selfish. This is self-preservation, Mom." I'm willing to help around the house and sometimes make dinner, but emotionally I created strict boundaries. I took the last sip of my coffee. "Will you please pass the coffee pot?"

Uncharacteristically, she gruffly shoves the pot, but it slides off the table and shatters on the floor, spraying hot coffee all over the floor and everything in the vicinity, including us.

"Now look what you did! These are my new linen pants."

"I didn't do it, but I'll help you clean it up."

She storms out of the kitchen as I survey the carnage and begin the slow process of sweeping the broken shards into a dustpan and mopping up the coffee. I love my mom, but her life makes me sad, especially her paralysis when it comes to her rotten husband. It is a cautionary tale.

CHAPTER 6
BROKEN APART

"An abuser isn't abusive 24/7. They usually demonstrate positive character traits most of the time. That's what makes the abuse so confusing when it happens, and what makes leaving so much more difficult."
-Miya Yamanouchi

With more boundaries in place between myself and my parents, I consciously decide to forgive my mom but realize it will take time to fully process my childhood. For years, I've carried disappointment and anger over her inability to protect me as a child. I believe she did the best she could. To move toward forgiveness, I write down three things: things I love about Mom, things I have worked on and forgive her for, and things I can't figure out and about which I need to know more.

My decision allows me to step into my adult self. In sorting out my childhood, I conclude that you can't pick your parents, and you certainly can't change them. I can only take charge of myself and the way I respond to my parents.

My new boundaries have a powerful impact on my relationship with Dad. The fear I harbor for my dad begins to dissipate. As a child, I was always afraid that he could hurt me and other family members, but as an adult, I know the power of my voice, and I am confident to use it. Dad is just someone who lives in the house; I have nothing to say to him, so I don't interact with him unless there's no one else. He's an ally of last resort.

I'm dating more and urge my dates to bring my mom a flower or small gift. If my date offers me a gift, I ask him to give it to her instead. "She'll love you for it!"

One night, a boy comes to pick me up and honks the horn.

My dad says, "Really, if he can't come in, he doesn't have any right dating you."

I agree, but I wonder, *is he possessive of me, or does he really think my date has no manners?*

My mom loves hearing the details about my dates. Because she loves gifts, she wants me to describe the gift giving. She "oohs" and "ahhs" over the way my dates held my hand. She rates them. She cares deeply about how boys treat me. She always says, "Never marry a man like your dad."

And I think, *you better believe I won't!*

She insists on feeding every boyfriend who visits. She has a special way of building relationships with them, drawing out details about their lives. It brings me joy because my mom is so social and thrives on my happiness when I'm with a good young man.

When I'm 19, my dad frequently travels to China and Africa for work. It's not until I'm 21 that my mom discloses to me in a depressed state that she found a five-inch stack of letters from various women in Africa and Asia. It turns out that my dad has no work projects in Africa. We all know he's traveling for leisure, but we don't realize until we discover the letters that he has romantic interests on two continents. My mom is heartbroken, which seems crazy to me.

I look at her like, *what the heck, Mom.*

She says, "Yes, but he loves us," and her face rests in resignation.

Our family heads to Canada for the summer to visit my dad's childhood friend, Carl, who owns a large property in the Yukon. He is a self-made millionaire who retired young and travels and builds homes there. He loves to invite friends from Germany and the US to stay in the vacation homes he built and go fishing. Because my dad and Carl were close childhood friends, our family began traveling to the Yukon when we lived in Arizona for summer hunting trips. I'm always the designated cook for the game and fish they catch. I find it odd that my dad never hunts; instead, he hikes or canoes. Ironically, he can't bear the thought of hurting an animal but never seemed to be bothered by hurting me.

During the frigid Canadian winters, Carl stays with us in Tacoma. We have a lifelong history with Carl and his family, from his up-bringing with my dad, to his mom staying with us in Arizona and reconnecting with him once we returned to the States.

During my 20th summer, Carl invites Mom to Alaska to make curtains for his yacht there and his nine vacation homes in Canada. Her job is initially scheduled for a few weeks but lasts the entire summer. Sonya and I realize that she has fallen in love with Carl. She's so happy with him. They adore and respect each other. They travel initially to get curtain material, but then later for pleasure.

One day, Mom calls me from Hawai'i to check in. "Hi, Cindy. Guess where we are?"

"I have no idea."

"We're in Hawai'i looking for curtain material."

Yeah, right. I laugh. I ask, "How are the curtains coming along?"

She giggles. "So great!"

The "curtain making" lasts for years.

Sometimes in front of my dad, I slip and mention that Carl came to town. I can tell by his wincing that he's jealous, but he trusts his old friend. My sister and I stay quiet about Mom and Carl because we've never seen Mom so happy. Carl takes her in his plane to remote places. I don't question her about the relationship because I know it brings her special joy. When they're in town, I adore watching Carl read to my mom. She holds his hand and gazes off into the distance, listening intently as he reads. Their relationship is based on true companionship and friendship. It is a beautiful thing to see my mom genuinely happy and at ease—at long last.

I ask mom if she's in love, and she says "maybe" with a mischievous grin.

Thank God she's finally doing something for herself.

One morning, I'm finishing homework at the kitchen table before school starts. Mom shuffles over to me and kisses my forehead in silence. She barely raises her voice from a whisper. "Hi." The corners of her mouth turn up; it's not exactly a smile—more like an upside-down frown.

She has been depressed for so many months that I've lost count. She hates Tacoma, the cold, and her empty, loveless relationship. Mom and Dad are back to their usual bickering. I can't stand it. I don't know how she can live like this. She says she has us to live for, but the pressure has become unbearable.

In her depressed zombie pace, she heads for the other side of the kitchen to get a medium-size mixing bowl and a whisk. Her terry cream slippers seem to be filled with lead, scuffing across the linoleum. With each shuffling step, I feel pity, anger, confusion, and love for her. *Where's the mom I once adored hiding?*

Sonya joins me at the table. "Good morning, Mom," she says perkily.

"I'm making some scrambled eggs for myself. Do you want some? You kids should eat something healthy," she says, flatly, lowering the cast-iron skillet onto the stovetop with a clang.

"Yes," Sonya and I say in unison.

Mom adjusts her quilted satin floral cream robe. The happy flowers contrast with her colorless aura. The light is gone from her face. She's just going through the motions, blind to the reality that only she can change her life. I wish I could give her faith that she would be okay if she leaves Dad. Why doesn't she start a life with Carl? If not him, her sisters invite her to live with them until she figures out what to do. She often says, "Time is precious, and remember that you can't buy time back." Yet, she does nothing but piss away the years.

Dad strolls in and says, "Good morning," pours a cup of coffee, then sits down with us.

The sizzling butter in the frying pan interrupts the silence. We pretend not to notice the discomfort of the zombie in the kitchen. It has become our norm.

It's perfectly normal to sit down with a pedophile for breakfast and have a catatonic zombie make us scrambled eggs—right?! When I'm stressed, I crack jokes in my mind to diffuse my tension. I smirk and wiggle in my seat at my twisted humor. I've read that people who've suffered trauma laugh to relieve tension in stressful situations. When I was younger, I would laugh out loud, but I've grown past that. I still suppress the urge to cry when I'm in pain, but someday, I hope to cry like a normal person in the face of hurt.

How do you help someone who won't help themselves? How can one ignore things as plain as day? Does she not think about these things? I feel mad just watching Mom shuffle and slump. I feel trapped right along with her.

Mom said she would leave Dad when we graduated from high school. My sister and I are both in college, so she's free to go! We act as go-betweens for Mom and Dad; we are victims trapped in our circumstance. I feel ashamed for thinking this way, but it's true. When do we get to live for ourselves? When is it our turn? I have so many mixed emotions. I want to help and support, yet I also want to run away and be completely indulgent like my friends, who don't have to babysit their parents.

Our family life has been so dysfunctional, which has knitted Sonya, Mom, and me into a tight threesome, but it's time to make decisions and transition away from our cocoon. Mom and Dad must pursue the life they chose, and Sonya and I must decide what we want to make of ours. Ugh! Transitions are always messy especially when it comes to matters of the heart. I don't even know how to start with so many layers of dysfunction. I need to let Mom know how I feel. She called me selfish. Maybe she really felt that way, or perhaps anger made her say it. But if selfish to her means taking care of myself, so be it!

I'd like to have another heart-to-heart conversation with her to understand her thinking. Last year, I was so upset when hearing her rationale for returning to Dad after the shelter when she had the chance to move in with her siblings. How is she okay living with an abuser, someone who criticizes everything she does, someone who makes her feel ugly and small? How does she live knowing he abused me physically, sexually, and mentally? What a fricking loser!

I found last year's heart-to-heart with Mom healing. I had to let go of the pain from the betrayal of a mother who didn't protect me. Even though I didn't agree with her, it offered closure and forgiveness.

Mom and I approach thinking differently. I believe human thought originates from three parts of our bodies: mind, heart, and gut. Most adults solely think with their minds, neglecting their heart and gut. Life lessons may teach us that the heart and the gut are based on feelings, which are fleeting. As a result, the mind is elevated above the other two, neglecting the fact that they work best together.

It seems that children think with their hearts first, their gut second, and then their heads. They forgive and love quickly as their heart directs their decisions. As a child, I relied on my gut—my intuition. My heart and head were at odds because I didn't trust what adults said. My intuition served me better. I ran at the first sign of trouble and saved thinking for later. As such, I may have overdeveloped my intuitive side; I often deeply feel other people's pain or troubles. I can be sensitive and find it difficult to be around negative people. I distrust people who aren't straightforward, and steer clear of those who I have trouble reading emotionally. My early trauma forced me to rely on my gut, which served me in the form of self-protection.

As an adult, I find that it's easy to get fixated on critical thinking loops and store that pain and grief in my body. I admire the beauty of a child's heart to quickly move past petty things. When children fall, they quickly get back up, dust themselves off, and move forward. Children always look for the next challenge without carrying the weight of their last fall. It's a reminder that it's a choice—not allowing one's mind to fill up with the "what ifs" or petty matters.

I try to think of this analogy and be conscious of not storing the grief I feel for Mom's ability to freeze when she faces decisions. She uses her head for decision-making only while her intuition slumbers. She second-guesses her choices even after they are made. With her pain bottled up, she tends to get physically ill from stress.

I discover that I can let go of stored pain and trauma through the toughest and most honest conversations. Mom has a greater understanding from my point of view and says it pains her to see how much anger I hold onto. I realize she is exactly right.

Forgiving another person has layers. Once I reach a layer, I need more explanation of the other person's point of view, even if I don't agree. That way, both perspectives are expressed respectfully. In that place, I find healing.

Questions remain about why Mom felt Dad would change after we returned from the shelter. Did she honestly believe him? Does she believe she did the right thing to live with a man she despises so Sonya and I would have a so-called good life? It makes no sense to me.

She needs to know that it's time I start living for myself. I can't live in this dysfunctional environment much longer, enabling Mom, and living a lie. I'm afraid of what she may say. I'm afraid it might make me angry.

I can't wait to leave this all behind. When you attempt to save a drowning person, if they try to pull you down with them, you must let go and save yourself.

CHAPTER 7
DOES THIS CHANGE EVERYTHING?

An unresolved issue will be like a cancer with the potential to spread into other areas of your relationship, eroding the joy, lightness, love, and beauty.
-Joyce Vissell

I've never been to Hawai'i, so I decide to go with my girlfriend, Milly, for my 21st birthday. We ride the escalator to the hotel lobby, excited to finally arrive after lots of planning and anticipation. A preppy guy passing in the opposite direction smiles, and I smile back. After we check into the hotel, the preppy man shares the elevator with us.

He says, "Wow! Check out your tan!"

I laugh. "I was kind of born with a tan."

When Milly and I reach our floor, he pauses the elevator. "Hey, a group of my buddies and I are going to the Moose tonight. Come join us! By the way, I'm Henry."

At the end of the evening, Milly and I do just that. He is nice but nervous talking to me, jittery, and wiggling his feet. He's cracking corny jokes.

I find it odd since it was just me. *Why would anyone be nervous? It's just me!* "Why are you nervous around me?"

"I'd like to see you again." He asks if I want another glass of wine.

"Rose, please."

As he walks off, Milly says, "Why are you talking to him? He doesn't seem right for you!"

My friend is a boho-style hippy, not at all into preppy guys, like Henry.

"I think he's nice."

Henry is the all-American boy I dreamt of while living overseas. He plays football and baseball and drives a cool Mazda RX-7 sports-car. He wears collared polo shirts with a turned-up collar and slings his Levi jacket over his shoulder. It's the fashionable bad boy look that Tom Cruise portrayed in the 80s. Henry graduated as an economics major and wants to be a stockbroker. He is ambitious and driven.

He's bright, loves a good time, and always treats me like a lady. My parents instantly like him, and I take to his family as well. We are young and love to have fun, but during our first year of dating, I prepare myself to share my history of sexual abuse. I trust him implicitly, so I feel like I can tell him. Henry is the first person I decide to share my history with. Even after I make the decision, I can't find the perfect time—on a drive, a walk, or in bed? When I realize there's no perfect time, I think, *I'll just go for it.*

One night as we settle into bed, I blurt, "I never told you this. My dad sexually and physically abused me."

He sits up, his eyes searching. "Like what?"

I suddenly feel as if I'm naked in a public area with a spotlight beaming on me and speaking into a loudspeaker. I want to rush through it. I rub my sweaty palms on my PJs. "He pushed me down the stairs at my grandmother's house in San Francisco."

Henry is furious. If he were a cartoon character, he'd have steam blowing out of his ears. He scrunches up his face in disgust. "That's terrible! Well, he's strange, but I don't like what he's done." He sighs. "I'll have to learn to accept him, I suppose. He is your father after all."

"I just wanted you to know." I'm worried he'll say, *we're never going to see your parents again.* What would I do then? "You can't share this with anyone else—okay?"

He nods and listens intently and doesn't pry but asks just enough questions to show he genuinely cares. I don't go into detail because talking about my sexual abuse is new and uncomfortable. Even though Henry is accepting, I feel vulnerable and ashamed that I haven't done a better job of working through my feelings.

We date for three years, and as our relationship progresses and as we build more trust, I share more details of the abuse. It is never easy, but the more I share, the more I shed pieces of the trauma. Sharing the memories with Henry allows the pain wrapped around them to dissipate and is freeing. One day, on a long drive, I decide to share the disturbing details of my dad's obsession with middle-of-the-night photo shoots.

In the dark of the night, my dad's stalky shadow appeared above me. He quietly tapped my shoulder to wake me. "Shh! Don't say a word." He held his hand out. And confused, I grabbed it. At seven years old, I still obey my dad. He led me into the hallway, and we paused outside my parents' bedroom. He closed the door ever so slightly, so my mom remained asleep. We tiptoed down the hall to his makeshift studio. He had positioned a barstool on a white sheet in the middle of the room and a white screen as a backdrop. He had set up a tripod with his Kodak Brown Twin 20 camera aimed toward the screen. A stool next to the tripod held the flashbulbs.

I wore pajamas my mom made for me, but I was chilly out from under my comfy bed covers. I wanted to return to the cozy warmth of my bed. As I stood there wondering what we were doing, my dad handed me white cotton bobby socks with lace trim. He pointed to my black Mary Janes that waited for me by the camera and asked me to put them on. He handed me a white cotton tank top and asked me to change into it. I stood still, half-dressed in my tank top, underwear, socks, and shoes. Goosebumps covered my arms and legs. All I wanted was to be warm and asleep next to my sister. He guided me to the barstool while he adjusted his camera. I was foggy headed, feeling like the whole scene was a dream.

He excitedly said, "You look so beautiful!" and took the first picture. The bright flash of the bulb roused me from my fogginess. "Okay, now put your hand behind your head and cross your legs like a lady."

I did as he asked, even though I felt silly.

"Okay, now smile!... Okay, now, don't smile!...Now that's my little girl!"

Click, click, click, the camera captured me. He asked me to get off the barstool and stand next to it, posing with my right foot in front and my left foot slightly turned out.

Then he asked me to take off my t-shirt and underwear. This was the first time he asked me to take naked photos, but because the routine of putting on my socks, shoes, and bow was familiar, the request didn't seem odd. When I complied without complaint, he scurried behind the camera and shrugged his shoulders with excitement, pumped with adrenaline. He could barely contain his excitement when he said, "Put your hand behind your head, like a lady! Now that looks good!... Now rest your hand on the top of the barstool... Okay, smile!...Okay, don't smile!"

I didn't understand the point of not smiling. *Wasn't I supposed to look happy?*

The flash turned a couple more times before the bulb needed to be changed. He paused and repositioned me. With a new bulb in place, the silent room filled again with flash, click, flash, click.

Each time the camera flashed, I was blinded for a second. I blinked to regain my sight.

"Have I ever told you how beautiful you are?" he asked.

I didn't say anything, but I felt pleased that he thought so.

He smiled. "Okay, we're all done!"

He instructed me to put on my nighty and leave my socks and Mary Janes near the camera where I had found them, and then he said, "Shh!" as he escorted me down the hallway. As we passed my parents' room, he gently pushed their door open to its original position. He tucked me back into bed, kissed me on the forehead, and whispered, "Don't tell your mother. It's just our secret. Okay?"

I nodded.

"You're so beautiful, and I love you so much. Now get some sleep."

What just happened? I wondered as I drifted off to sleep.

85

Henry shakes his head while keeping his eyes on the road. "Cindy, that's seriously twisted," he says shaking his head. "He's one warped dude. I mean, how can you even have a relationship with him?"

"I suppose it wasn't all bad." I pull my legs up to my chest and wrap my arms around them, hypnotized by the ribbon of highway.

"Right. But the bad *way* outweighs the good."

"I don't know. I guess I'm trying to figure out how to navigate this while living my life."

He quickly glances over at me.

Does he see me differently now? Does he think I'm damaged? Maybe I shouldn't have shared so much.

"I'm surprised you're not more messed up."

"Oh, I'm plenty messed up. I just hide it well," I laugh. "Henry?" I say, my voice tinged with worry.

"Yes?"

"Does this change everything?"

"What do you mean?"

"I mean, how you see me?"

When he understands what I'm asking, he takes my left hand in his and tenderly kisses it. "No way. No way does it change everything. It changes nothing."

I worry that Henry won't be able to deal with my dad after this revelation. But he remains polite around him and doesn't seem to judge him or his interactions with me. He stays neutral, even though I couldn't if I were in his shoes. In private, I refer to my dad as a weirdo, and we joke about him, but Henry never disparages him unless I take the lead.

After three years of dating, when I'm 25 and Henry is 26, we marry. A year into our marriage, we welcome our sweet baby girl, Hannah. Mom is a godsend; she sometimes stays with us for weeks. She adores her first grandchild and is the baby whisperer. She teaches me so much about motherhood and nurturing a baby. She shares her wisdom, and I appreciate her companionship.

In the meantime, Henry approaches me about wanting to open a bar with pool tabs—legalized gambling—where the house usually wins. He says there are risks associated with it, such as alcoholism, infidelity, and gambling. But I trust him with my life. I truly believe we won't become a grim statistic.

Two years later, when pregnant with our son, Brian, Mom comes to the rescue again. She helps with Hannah, housework, and cooking, and she keeps me company. She loves to place her hands on my growing stomach, lean in, hold her mouth close, and have one-sided conversations with Brian in utero while I rest on the couch. She said she talked to me when I was in the womb, which is why I knew so much about the world at such a young age. I count on her help, affection, and ability to bring light to any situation.

I love to picture my mom when I was a baby, admiring me for my Cindy-ness, in awe of every toothless smile. Although she didn't always protect me as a child, I know she loved me and showed me as often as she could. She had limitations and fears that prevented her from being an executive decision-maker in her marriage, health, and the well-being of her children. She often notes that our approaches to problem-solving are radically different.

My rollercoaster feelings of love and anger are a natural response to feeling betrayed. I try to let go of my judgment and focus on her love. However, if I had been in my mom's shoes, I would have taken my children and left my husband for our safety and well-being. I wouldn't have hesitated to start all over again. This doesn't make me better, simply different from my mom. I'm learning to let go of her shortcomings and love all the wonderful things she gave me. Forgiveness and acceptance are the only path forward in our relationship.

As my mom helps me care for our home during my pregnancy, she jokingly says, "Your dad is getting the best of me! He's killing me!" She always said this in jest when we were kids. Once again, she reminds me of Edith in the *Archie Bunker* show as she nods her head, but this time, I feel a deeper resonance. They are both passive and a bit clueless. Because they only want to see the best in people, their perception is clouded by denial.

Mom complains of strange ailments. She struggles with migraines, carpal tunnel syndrome, hair loss, and arthritis. She develops calcifications on her spine and neck that limit her range of motion. She goes from one doctor visit to the next, feeling worn out. She wears neck and hand braces to alleviate the pain. She resists the recommended medications and therapy because she doesn't trust physicians and spends days in pain. My dad is emotionally distant and absent, traveling between the US and China for work. It pains me to see her so miserable, unhappy, and alone.

As Mom struggles with her health, I deliver our son, Brian. He's a whopping 10 lbs. 9 oz.! The OB/GYN projected him to be 7 lbs., so his size comes as a complete surprise. Henry and I are delighted beyond words to have a son. My mom stays with us for a month to help transition to two kids, even as she continues to suffer. She feels better staying with us and watching Hannah play gives her incredible joy. My mom adores Hannah's every word and is amused by her sassiness and frequent use of the word "no."

Is that a grandma thing? I don't remember her admiring me when I said "no" as a child.

One evening, after we put the kids to bed, Mom and I curl up on the couch next to each other while sipping beers. I'm dog tired but need time to unwind before heading to bed. Mom downs her beer quickly and is uncharacteristically giggly. I join in, even though I don't know what we're laughing about. She jumps up to get another beer. "Want another?" she asks.

"Oh, no thanks. I'm only halfway through my first."

She sinks into the couch with her second beer, which she downs like she's got a quenchless thirst.

"Mom, you're going to drink me under the rug tonight."

She laughs. "So, Cindy…"

"Yes?"

"I have some news. Some big news."

"Oh, yeah?" I can't imagine what her news might be. *Is she moving? Starting a new job?*

 "I'm divorcing your father," she says, barely able to contain her excitement. She looks like a little girl on Christmas morning. I can't remember the last time she looked so alive. She beams, and her eyes sparkle as she reaches toward me for a hug.

I've waited for these words my entire life, and to see her finally step into her power brings me to tears. We hold each other as I sob on her shoulder.

"Are you sad, sweetie?" she asks.

I lift my head and hold her gaze. "Are you kidding me? This is the happiest moment of my life!"

"Phew! I was worried."

She shares her dreams of falling in love all over again, of finding companionship with a new man. We strategize about where she will live, her financial situation, and the legal process. We clink our beer bottles at least 30 times, toasting every part of her plan and each brave step she to get there. I'm overjoyed to see her full of light and hope for a new life.

CHAPTER 8
BAD THINGS COME IN THREES

"When things fall apart, they are actually realigning."
-Molly M. Cantrell-Kraig

My sweet baby boy is special and unique. He never cries, never complains; he's so happy, alert, and very bright. I've heard many horror stories about difficult babies. I feel blessed to have such an angelic child.

That feeling doesn't last long, though. After a month, I sense something's wrong. When cradling my baby in our living room, I say to Henry, "There's something behind his left eye."

Henry leans in, looks, and shakes his head. "Nah. There's nothing." I can tell he thinks I'm crazy and imagining things.

"Can't you see that his eye is slightly elevated?" Tears stream down my face in mourning for my perfect baby boy.

Henry strokes Brian's cheek and then gently touches my shoulder. "Sweetie, I think you need to get some rest."

Despite Henry and everyone else reassuring me, I won't let it go. I take Brian to our pediatrician. "There's something behind his left eye. Can't you see his eye protruding? I truly believe there's something behind his left eye."

The pediatrician eyes me with skepticism. It's the same look Henry gives me whenever I express my concerns. "I can't give a referral because you have a hunch."

"It's more than a hunch. Trust me. I've gazed at his face for hundreds of hours since he was born."

The doctor gives me a referral to a pediatric optometrist, who says he sees a shadow in the back of Brian's eye and thinks an MRI is a good idea.

At Seattle Children's Hospital, Henry and I hesitate to hand our two-month-old baby boy to the MRI technician. I don't want to hand him over. If I hold onto him, I won't pass him off to the cruel hands of fate where mothers can't protect their baby boys. In my arms, I'll keep him safe and healthy forever. I plead to go to the MRI room with him, but the technician says we must wait here. I imagine Brian slipping into the dark tube of doom without his mama.

I try to calm myself in the waiting room with positive thoughts, prayers, and mantras, but nothing works. The things people have said to me play over and over in my mind. *It's all going to be okay. You're just imagining things. Everything's going to work out.*

Henry leans forward, resting his heavy head in his hands. Although we're next to each other, we feel worlds apart.

The room fills up with strangers, and I wonder what terrible news awaits them in the room of doom.

A nurse in drab grey scrubs approaches us with a grave expression. The minute I see her long face, I know. She passes Brian to me, and I pull him in close.

"What is it?" I blurt out.

"Please come with me," she says.

"What? What's wrong?" I ask. I hate the protocols that prevent underlings from sharing bad news with patients. We trod down the hygienic hall with nurses and doctors scurrying past.

"I'll have you speak with the radiologist."

Hold it together. Just hold it together until we get home.

The radiologist introduces herself with a warm smile and invites us to sit in a claustrophobic room with an overpowering scent of chemical disinfectant. My gaze goes immediately to the MRI images on the screen. My baby boy's brain appears in dark grey with folds with a white splotch behind his eye.

It's. A. Tumor.

My heart races, and my head spins.

The radiologist sits next to me and catches my eye. "How did you know?" she asks.

"It's a tumor, right?" I ask, praying that I'm wrong.

She sits next to me. "Yes. It must be mother's intuition. The tumor grew in utero and is the size of a walnut and located in the frontal part of his brain."

A week later, a nurse escorts Henry, Hannah, and I into a white examining room where we wait for the neurosurgeon. We are there to discuss how they will remove Brian's tumor and learn what to expect for his future.

Two built-in navy vinyl benches line the room. Hannah slowly tiptoes the length of the longest bench. Her toes indent the vinyl as she hums a made-up song in childlike bliss. She goes back and forth, repeating the same tiptoed steps, humming all the while.

Usually, I can get lost in her world of wonder. Today, the contrast of her world and my world is too great—the chasm too wide.

Henry nervously bounces his leg, one crossed over the other. He shifts legs, repeating his nervous twitch, audibly sighs, and glances at the clock every few minutes. I sit on the long bench against the wall to give Hannah room to roam while nursing Brian on and off.

I'm numb, disconnected from the truth of Brian's diagnosis. I can't face the reality until I hear all the facts. Henry carries so much anxiety, grief, and fear while I live in the moment. I wait for the facts so I can go to a quiet space to digest them and tend to my grief.

The chief neurosurgeon, Dr. Mitch Berger, bursts into the room with a team of five doctors and a couple of residents in tow. I listen in shock as he lays out his plan with a booming voice. Henry covers his face in anguish as the surgeon describes Brian's surgery that would be performed in a year. It pains me to witness his distress. I'm not sure how to console him, either. We have endured stress before, but nothing could have prepared us for this. I have very few questions, unlike Henry, who peppers the surgeon with questions.

I quickly go through a list of my concerns as the doctor goes through his. Who will take care of Hannah while I'm in the hospital? How will Hannah get to her play group to see her friends? Henry works nights and can't do both. How long will I go back and forth to Seattle Children's hospital? A month? A year? A lifetime?

Dr. Burger says during the first procedure, they will determine the type of tumor and that Brian's odds of living are 50 percent.

"Excuse me. Did I hear that right? 50 percent?" Henry says, almost angrily.

"Yes, that's right."

They haven't even begun the surgery, and his odds are 50-50! My son could die. He's only two months old and still feels like he is growing inside me. I want to take my baby boy and his sister and run far, far away from this place. Crushing fear overtakes my body; the pain in my heart is acute, as if an arrow pierced it. I negotiate with the black cloud of fear—*please retreat to so I can hear and process the doctor's words.* I will the surgeon to spit out the information more quickly so I wouldn't get stuck in fear.

I go through my laundry list to distract myself from the fear growing inside me. *I guess Hannah's play dates are going bye-bye. I'll have to cancel our Hanukkah party. How can I possibly be a good mother to Hannah, a wife, fill myself with what I need, and be there for Brian? Oh my gosh! In the stress of getting here, I forgot to pack a snack for Hannah. It has already begun. Chaos!* I want to slap myself over these thoughts. I don't know how to digest the devastating news.

The surgeon says the longer they can postpone the first procedure, the odds of him surviving would be greater. One major concern is potential loss of blood since Brian is a baby and will not have enough blood supply to survive the surgery.

My thoughts turn to our household. *I must make our home as stable and normal as possible be for our family over the upcoming holidays and Christmas.* I feel so mechanical about my thought process yet fully informed of his medical diagnosis.

The doctor turns to me. "Do you have any questions? You've been a little quiet."

Yeah, is my boy going to live? If he lives, will he be disabled? And if he doesn't live, how can I go on? "I have all the information I can handle at this point."

"What's going through your mind?"

"Fear. It looks like I will have to cancel Hanukkah."

Henry and the doctor do a doubletake.

Oh, my God, did I really say that out loud? Seriously, tell me I'm dreaming! "I'd be concerned if I heard that, too. I handle stress oddly and sometimes with terrible humor. I've always been this way." I'm sure it's from my early and sustained trauma. I decide not to say anything more.

He says bluntly, "Okay. Well, then, I will set you up with a social worker to help you through this."

When we get home, Henry shares Brian's next steps with family and friends. I can barely talk about it and find myself comforting others, who cry with the news.

In just two months, the tumor doubles in size—from the size of a large grape to an orange—and the neurosurgeon recommends that they operate immediately. The doctors were not anticipating the rapid growth of the tumor and decide to operate at four months old. It is not a year later like we were hoping for. Brian's odds of surviving are slim. He is the first infant to have ever been born with this type of rare brain tumor.

My world stops, and I fall into the darkest depression imaginable. I've never encountered frozen grief where it feels like my mind, heart, and body have stopped in space. For a week, I lie in a dark room and can't let go of Brian. I constantly nurse him, terrified of the thought of never holding him again, angry that I may not be able to watch him grow into manhood. I want the sound of his sleeping breath to be embedded in my memory if I never hear it again. I want to hold onto every second imaginable. My days are a blur of nursing, crying, sleeping, and Mom silently coming into the room to change Brian's diaper and feed me.

After a week of grief so intense it almost consumes me, my mother sits next to me and gently shakes my shoulder to awaken me. She says it is time to get back to the real world. I had slept for a week and had responsibilities to meet. I can't believe I slept an entire week! It feels like it was like 24 hours. I emerge from my dark bedroom and am greeted with a giant hug from Hannah.

"Oh, Mama, I'm so glad you're all better now."

From darkness into light, I walk to her bedroom, where she shows me how she arranged the stuffed animals by size and explains how they were waiting for me.

This period becomes the darkest time of my entire life. Time stops for days. I'm emotionally frozen with the news. We're at the mercy of our doctors and science.

While attending a support group meeting for children with brain tumors, I learn that 92 percent of parents divorce due to the stresses of having a child with severe medical issues. It's so upsetting. I can't fathom surviving this experience without my husband. I vow that Henry and I will be among the eight percent of couples that survive. I'm very much in love with him, and the notion of divorce is unthinkable.

When in Brian's hospital room the day before his first surgery, the little guy hooked up to a million monitors, I share my fears with Henry, adding that whatever disagreements we have, we need to pull ourselves together for our kids and our marriage, maybe even see a therapist.

The light drains from his eyes, and his face hardens. "There's no way I'm going to therapy."

Brian's heart rate monitor beeps incessantly in the background. Each beep feels like a warning, a reminder that his fragile life is on the line, as if each beep could be the last. I watch the red second dial on the clock go around a few times. I want to shake my husband and say, *Don't you see what's at stake? Don't you want to save our marriage? Our sweet little family? Ourselves?* I focus on my breath to calm my panic, realizing that I can't force the issue. He is so caught up in grief that counseling won't happen now, maybe never. I ask him to stay with our boy while I talk to the social worker, who later mentors me. I ask her to add me to the list for individual counseling. I have no control over what is to come of my son or my marriage, but just maybe I can find a way to save myself.

The outcome of Brian's surgery and the prognosis are unknown. We must trust that the surgery will work and decide to take the chance. What other options do we have?

We spend the night in Brian's room, and our sweet little boy is wheeled out of the room before dawn. I wake up from my fitful hospital-room sleep just long enough to kiss him on the cheek and whisper, "Mama loves you."

Henry and I pace and slouch, drink too much hospital coffee, and eat too many salty, sugary vending machine snacks. Running on sugar, caffeine, nerves, and exhaustion, we jump up when the surgeon appears in his scrubs, his mask resting beneath his smile.

"Your boy was a champ! We successfully removed the tumor."

I clutch Henry's arm in glee but also to steady myself. "Oh, my goodness! What a relief!"

"Come with me," the surgeon says, with a sudden heaviness in his voice.

I want him to linger on his triumphant news for a few minutes longer. We follow him down the hallway toward post-op.

"The tumor was lodged in the left frontal part of Brian's brain, so to completely remove it, we had no choice but to remove his speech and emotional centers. The tumor had grown through the optic nerves, so to excise the remaining parts of the tumor, we severed his optic nerves. Unfortunately, he will lose sight in and movement of his left eye. He also required a blood transfusion. The good news is he had a higher survival rate because he's larger and had more blood supply than a smaller infant."

I feel faint, unsteady on my feet. I stop for a minute and lean against the wall for support. *What does this mean? Our boy will live, but he won't be able to speak, process emotions, or see out of his left eye? He may never live a normal life! He may always be dependent on us!* I don't know what to feel—happy because he survived, since the tumor is gone, but devastated because essential parts of his brain went with it.

"Are you okay?" asks Henry.

"I'm not sure," I say, resting my head against the wall.

"Take a moment. I know it's a lot to take in," says the surgeon.

I nod. *You've got that right. You can just walk away from our boy. As his mom, I will live with the consequences.*

During the most intense six months of Brian's health crisis, my mom discovers a lump in her breast a few weeks after she filed for a divorce. She says it's the stress from Dad moving out and hopes it will go away. Two weeks later, she notices the lump is quite large but continues with her move and prepares to put the house on the market. By the time she finally sees a doctor, a month and a half have passed since she first discovered the lump.

One day, Mom shares that she has an aggressive form of breast cancer that has spread throughout her breast. The doctors want to operate immediately, but she freezes in indecision. She is committed to naturopathic medicine and is against chemotherapy. She also refuses to have a mastectomy. She says, "No man will ever love someone without a breast or who has ugly scars in place of a breast!"

It is nearly impossible to understand her thinking, and honestly, it infuriates me. I want to say, *no man will ever love you if you're dead.* But, of course, I keep my thoughts to myself.

She delays addressing her issue to gather more opinions. Her fear overwhelms her. I try to problem solve and take her to different doctors, but the more input she gets, the more she freezes in analysis paralysis.

At the same time, Brian is undergoing more incredibly risky procedures, and it baffles Mom that I can quickly make health decisions. She questions his experimental drugs and surgeries and reminds me that he is only a baby.

She challenges my confidence in the doctors, asking, "How do you know Brian will be all right?"

"Mom, I never know if he's going to be okay, but I have to try. Don't I? If it means going to ten doctors who say something's impossible, I'll go with the eleventh doctor who offers the possible option. Faith in medicine is really all I have!"

When the doctors quote me a 20 percent success rate for Brian's surgery, Mom is in disbelief. "How can you possibly do this?"

"Twenty percent is better than nothing. It's better than letting him die." I know this isn't comforting to her, but it's the reality.

She pushes a strand of hair from my face and smiles softly. "I've always admired the fight in you. It's something I've never known how to do. I'll support any medical decisions you make for Brian despite our different philosophies."

"I'll do the same for you," I promise, knowing it will be a challenge. I suspect her passivity will come back to haunt her.

Brian struggles after his major brain surgery. He goes into the ICU, and we sleep on the floor in the hospital on blow-up mattresses with 20 other parents. Sometimes we hear the people softly crying. The room is a stress and worry chamber.

Racked by worry, I finally fall asleep only to have a nurse shake my shoulder. "Wake up, Cindy. You need to come be with your son right now."

Even in my half-awake state, I know she's saying, you need to say goodbye. It strikes me if I go to him, he might not pull through. "No, I don't think I'm going to."

My baby boy makes it through another night.

Despite struggling with her health, Mom stays with me and helps with the kids. Sometimes, she gets up in the middle of the night when Brian fusses and gives him a bottle to quiet him back to bed. As her health declines, she prepares meals, and we make time to talk after putting the kids down. I'm grateful to have my mother there, even though we are both nearly stressed to the breaking point.

At first, Mom tries to hide her cancer with turtlenecks and button-up blouses, but she eventually opts for more comfortable clothing. The first time she wears a low scoop-neck T-shirt, I exclaim at the black web of cancer spidering up her neck. I ask if she'll show me the rest underneath her shirt. She reluctantly agrees. The cancer is visible on her sternum, breast, and the lower part of her rib cage.

At night, I help my vibrant, wiggly three-year-old into her pajamas and then tuck her into bed as she chatters on about how she wants all her toys arranged in her bed. I kiss her goodnight as she bosses her misbehaving dolls and animals. I put my baby boy into his pajamas and give him seizure medication through a syringe that I squirt into the back of his mouth. When he howls at the bitter taste, I nurse him for comfort, careful not to touch his sutures from a recent surgery. Afterward, I walk down the hallway and pop in to say goodnight to my mom and see if she wants something to ease her pain. She rarely complains, but I know she is suffering. When my beloveds are tucked in and sound asleep, I call Henry to check in and say goodnight. I can sense the strain and growing distance in our relationship. *How much longer will our marriage hold?* We rarely talk in person, often just passing in the night. The tavern we own in Federal Way closes at 2 am, so he gets home by 3 am. Although he needs to work long hours so the business runs smoothly, work has become a form of escapism, but I don't have the emotional bandwidth to work on our marriage. I just hope it holds long enough to get us through the crises.

Henry begins to drop weight, has frequent nosebleeds, and is acting strangely. One minute, he's anxious and paranoid; the next minute, he has crazy bursts of happiness. He is frequently angry and confrontational with the doctors, claiming they're not listening. It gets so bad the head neurosurgeon bans him from the main floor of the hospital.

He talks incessantly about eight-balls, and I wonder why he's so obsessed with pool balls. I hear gossip of Henry and the attractive female bartenders we hired, but Henry claims people are just trying to sabotage him. I don't ask why. I want to believe every word he utters.

I have incredibly detailed recurring dreams that he's having an affair. One morning, I share my dream with him. "Her name is Mary, and she's Asian from Vancouver. She has long brown hair."

"You're crazy," he says and yanks the covers over his head, turning away from me.

Three things are dying in front of me, and there's nothing I can do about it. Although I'm only 29, I feel like I'm 116, having already lived a lifetime.

CHAPTER 9
A DOUBLE LIFE

"One's dignity may be assaulted, vandalized and cruelly mocked,
but it can never be taken away unless it is surrendered.
-Michael J. Fox

My mom decides to receive treatment from a naturopathic clinic in Rosario, Mexico, and travels back and forth. I spend my days carting Brian to Seattle Children's Hospital. With each prolonged seizure, I worry that Brian will have permanent brain damage. Because he has so many seizures, we follow a protocol; we only call an ambulance if his seizure lasts longer than six minutes. His longest seizure lasts 20 minutes! I quickly call a neighbor to watch Hannah while I ride with Brian in the ambulance, not knowing how long I will be away. I feel horribly guilty, constantly leaving Hannah with friends and family. There are times I have no idea what's going on at the house because I'm in crisis mode at the hospital, dealing with Brian's seizures or surgery complications.

One morning, after a difficult night of seizures, the lead doctor recommends that Brian be permanently institutionalized. "He'll have nursing care with a support system," he promises.

105

Every part of me trembles. I hold onto the door to steady myself. Even though my boy uses a GI tube and can't see or walk, I say, "Brian's going to live through this. He's going to high school. He's going to college. If you don't have the vision, no one will have the vision," I proclaim. The strength of my resolve even surprises me.

I start saying "no" to doctors who don't resonate with my vision and am determined to pick my dream team of doctors. This is when I discover Dr. Steven Glass, a neurologist who works at Seattle Children's Hospital, the most inspiring of all the doctors.

I say to Dr. Glass, "Do you have patients who have pulled through this?"

"Yes, I do," he says with conviction. "Yes, I do."

These are the words I've waited to hear, and I clutch them to my heart like a promise.

During this difficult time, not only does Dad offer no support, but he also moves to Kauai thousands of miles away. We don't talk often, but when we do, he cries when I share news of Mom's or Brian's health. Instead of being helpful, he asks philosophical questions like, "Why would this happen to a child?"

It annoys me to no end because, once again, it's about his discomfort. He doesn't ask how Brian is feeling or about the rest of our family. When the conversation gets too heavy, he abruptly excuses himself. Why would I expect anything different? I know who he is—an intractable narcissist. Even though he will never change, I periodically remain in contact with him. I have unfinished business with him, and until I've worked through it, I won't cut him off. I need to do this to stay true to myself.

When my mom passes away a year after her diagnosis, I'm devastated. Although I knew her time was short, I wasn't prepared for the breathless heartbreak. I think, *God, why are you punishing me by taking Mom and not Dad?*

The only bright spot is Brian's health. The doctors feel he is out of the woods and will only improve over time. I pray they're right.

Shortly after my mom passes, just as I'm gaining momentum in my life, Sonya and a friend sit me down. Their grave expressions concern me.

What's wrong? What terrible thing happened?

They replay voicemail messages they saved on a recorder. My mom and a girlfriend listened to the messages when I was in the hospital with Brian. The messages are from female bartenders looking for Henry, some legitimate work messages, others asking for a hookup time. He apparently failed to mention he was married.

My first response is disbelief and denial. "Surely, there has been a mistake. Maybe these are just employees." I can't imagine Henry stepping out on our marriage while navigating Brian's health issues and my mom's death. As excuses and explanations swirl in my mind, my friend explains that my mom had been erasing messages meant for Henry.

Sonya married not long after I had wed, and her husband worked part-time at the bar during med school. My sister explains that he saw things that made him question Henry's relationships with the cocktail waitresses.

"Why didn't you tell me earlier?" My eyes dart between Sonya and my friend's faces for answers.

"We talked about it and decided you couldn't handle one more thing."

"But…"

I realize they were right.

That day, I dig through Henry's receipts and files. I find hotel receipts in his nightstand drawer. I dig further and go to our travel agent to investigate the travel receipts. After she prints out all the receipts for the year, I head to my car and slide into the driver's seat. I discover that his "fishing trips" had never happened; instead, he had gone to Las Vegas, having always purchased a companion seat. I rest my head on the steering wheel and cry until my eyes sting. I have a throbbing headache from the purge of tears. My palms ache from slapping the steering wheel in fury as I reflect on the good and bad times with Henry. I look down at the open file of messy paperwork that I threw up in the air in my fit of despair—hotel receipts, copies of travel receipts, a brown bag of horse racing track stubs, and a slew of bank statements. Honestly, I have no real proof of what Henry did in our marriage. I have assumptions, but that's all they are. What I do see is that our marriage deteriorated some time ago and we are irrevocably broken. We have no conflict resolution skills. Mom felt that for a relationship to survive, one needed a language for love and one for conflict. A silly saying from her plays in my head. *Eventually you need to face your weaknesses before they find you.* I'd dismiss her every time she said it because I was too young to understand. I reach over, grab the bag of horse racing receipts, and throw handfuls of betting stubs in the air. *Well said, Mama!* I scatter more in the air. Driving home pissed off, I think of the confetti parade. It might just be my parade to celebrate being divorced and single.

Then I'm oddly in a place of calm. *No one will be in this passenger seat for a long, long time.*

I head straight to the bank and discover that Henry had been taking cash advances on my credit cards. I'm horrified. I leave finances up to him and rarely look at our bank statements. I then discover that he had used our house as collateral for the bar.

I want to go home, crack open a beer, and sleep it off. Maybe when I wake up, I'll realize it is all a bad dream. Instead, the first thing I do is leaf through the Yellow Pages and call attorneys who can meet me before I change my mind.

I don't want to live in this lie for another day. I won't let myself. I'm not even 30. I refuse to lead a compromised life!

I know this is the beginning of a firestorm and lifestyle change, but I remind myself that I have the tenacity to endure whatever it takes. Although I'm devastated and at my lowest point, I must rally and pick myself up. This is another new beginning.

I can't live in the past. Mom's gone, and I will grieve for her later. I must stop living in fear and believe that Brian will be okay. I have no idea what I'll do financially and don't know where I'll live, but I can't let fear compromise my values.

With these thoughts and a strong resolve, I close the door to my marriage.

I wait a week to confront Henry. I need time to collect my thoughts and to garner the strength to hold it together. I need to know what he is thinking.

I suggest to Henry that we meet up at our favorite Mexican restaurant. It's brightly lit, so not at all romantic, and the friendly staff will help with the heavy, awkward moments I anticipate. The food always comes out quickly, which will be useful in case we want a quick exit strategy.

I think two weeks should be enough time to make up our minds if we're going to move past his indiscretions and to decide if we have enough love for each other to stay married. If you can't decide after two weeks of soul searching, then it probably isn't going to happen.

I assume Henry has been in the process of figuring out where he stands in our relationship for years before he started having affairs. He likely knows what he wants, and I need to hear his truth. I will base my decision on how our meeting goes. I'm very much in love with him and can't dismiss our years of happiness. I can envision establishing a new relationship with him through the guidance of counseling and deep heart-to-heart conversations. I know some relationships can be repaired after infidelity and become even healthier than before. My heart is broken, but we've gone through unsurmountable stress. I can't throw away all the good years based on poor decisions. People screw up and are fallible. Life gets messy, and we do dumb things, hurtful things, but you just don't give up on something good. I even surprise myself in the way I handle extreme stress. Sometimes I wonder who I am. However, preparing for the possibility that Henry may not want to reconcile, I sought out an attorney to determine my financial standing and to learn about the process of filing for a divorce. I weigh everything before our meeting.

When Henry strolls into the restaurant, he is reluctant to chat. I have the menu open on the table, and the waiter comes over right as Henry sits down.

"I'll just have a Coke," mumbles Henry to the waiter.

"I'll have a veggie taco," I say, trying to sound upbeat.

"No food for you?" the waiter asks Henry.

"Oh, I guess I'll have a beef burrito," he says as if someone is making him do it.

The waiter darts away with our orders.

"So, did you do it out of despair?" I ask.

His jaws jut out as he clenches his teeth. After a few minutes without him acknowledging my question, I try another.

"When did this start?" I ask, taking a long sip of water.

"Geez, Henry. Were you ever happy with me?" I say, grasping my water glass with both hands and bringing it to my mouth. I need both hands because I'm trembling.

He nods halfheartedly and stuffs his mouth with tortilla chips. He seems impatient with my questions.

"I wonder if you thought I was a good wife." I search his eyes for the answer because it's clear he's reluctant to respond to any of my questions.

He picks at his burrito while I inhale my entire taco with a knot in my stomach. I don't even taste it.

Henry says, "Okay, so I've got an offer for you. We can live together and raise the children in one household, but I'll continue to see other women. I'll pay for everything until we've raised the kids."

Seriously? That's your offer? It feels like a cold slap in the face. Although I had concluded that he knew what he wanted, this comes as a complete surprise. He got caught. Otherwise, we could have gone on like this forever.

I honestly want to run out of the restaurant and never look back, but instead, I stare down at the half-eaten bowl of tortilla chips.

Finally, he says, "Here's the thing, I don't find you attractive. I actually want someone younger."

I'm 29. How young do you want her to be? 21?

"Not only that. You're stupid and don't have a funny bone in your body."

Ouch! He's being downright mean and ugly. I hear his truth, and it stinks. I don't have much to say. "Well, I'm far too young to compromise my life while continuing this charade. I'd be living a lie, which would never work for me."

I slide my attorney's business card toward him and get up. I don't even say goodbye.

Our decisions have been made. I head home, cram all his crap into two suitcases while crying, and set them outside the door. I call a locksmith to change the locks.

So begins my life as a single mom.

I must save my intense grieving for another time when I have the time to process it slowly. If I allow myself to mourn, it will hold me in place, and fear will prevent me from going forward. Plus, if I'm overcome by grief, who will be strong for my children?

Each day, I jot down a to-do list. It's a mechanical process, but it reminds me to make time for everything, including my emotional well-being. It includes things like play with my kids, 30 minutes to cry and wallow in grief, clean the house, find out how much equity is in the house, find a realtor, and talk to a friend.

My daily to-do list allows me to move ahead, grieve, and be in the present. It allows me to be in control when so much is out of my control.

My children help me focus on what really matters. Even though I may not be in the mood, if my daughter says, "Look, Mommy!" and shows me her doll, I tune into her happiness and awe. It helps

112

me realize the amazing beauty that is mine. In those moments, life is so magical, and I value being present and grateful for what I have instead of regretting what I lack.

Shortly after Henry and I divorce, my sister moves to Plains, Montana, where her husband landed a job. It had been incredibly helpful to have her in town with the support of a brother-in-law who's a doctor. I struggle even more in their absence.

The kids and I live in our home while I plan our next steps. I know our lifestyle will change, but I don't yet realize to what extent.

CHAPTER 10
MAIL-ORDER MOM

"The need for control always comes from someone that has lost it."
-Shannon L. Alder

One day, my dad calls out of the blue. I'm sipping freshly brewed coffee at the kitchen counter, watching the kids play. It's my favorite moment of the day when I pause and enjoy my coffee before the world starts spinning out of control.

"Hi, Cindy! Guess what?"

"What, Dad?"

"You're not going to believe it."

"Try me." I figure he's got news about a job or moving back to the Mainland.

"I just married a lady in China."

I spew my sip of coffee all over the counter and try to conceal my laughter. He's right. I don't believe it.

"Cindy, are you still there?"

"Yes!" It feels comical. I don't know what to say. *Congratulations? Aren't there any women in Kauai? Is she an official mail-order bride? Are you in love with her?* I settle on, "How is that possible when you live in Kauai?" I don't say it enthusiastic, but perhaps he won't notice.

He said he'd reached out to a contact in China, explaining that he was recently divorced and looking for a new wife. That person connected him with a family from a rural village. He flew to China with a dowry to meet the family and daughter. He married her and brought her back to Hawai'i.

"Do they know how old you are?"

He attempts to avoid the question by talking about a recent flood in Kauai.

I don't let him off the hook. "Dad, did tell them your age?"

He sighs. "Yes, to marry someone older is an honorable thing because it brings more wisdom to the family."

I can't hold it in, "That's the biggest crock of shit I have ever heard!"

He laughs, which is a good sign. At least he's not completely delusional.

I don't have anything else to add, so he ends the conversation by saying they plan to travel to Seattle for their honeymoon and want to stop by. Most would find it odd that they waited a year later to take their honeymoon, but I don't since everything he does is odd and makes no sense. I'm surprised that stopping to visit me is part of their honeymoon.

I hang up the phone, already filled with dread over meeting my dad's mail-order bride, who is probably my age. Then it hit me. *She's my stepmom.* I shake my head. *My dad, the weirdo. Some things never change.*

When my dad and his new wife come to town a year later, I have a moment of insanity and agree to meet them at the airport. With the kids in daycare, I drive to the pick-up line at the airport, anticipating meeting my new mail-order stepmother. As I pull up to the arrival area, I see my dad on the sidewalk with a very young woman. Her body type is like mine. She has slender legs and arms and is a few inches shorter than me. She had thick, short, brown hair. Her high cheekbones and sunned skin tone remind me of Mom.

As I introduce myself, I notice her polite smile beneath her sad eyes. She bows toward me and nods her head a couple of times. She wears old, faded jeans, and a faded T-shirt. My dad notices me looking at her clothes and jokes that she dressed to look poor, hoping I would give her some of my clothes. It is a bizarre comment, but before I can respond, they climb into my car. I don't know what I would say anyway. *Dad, are you such a cheapskate that you don't buy your bride clothing?* Then I have more sinister thoughts that I push away.

A few minutes after leaving the airport, my dad says, "You can call her 'mother.'"

I shoot him a dirty look in the rearview mirror. "I will not call her 'mother.'" The fact that my dad suggested this disgusts me.

He laughs.

"I'm glad you find that funny."

His wife sits in the passenger seat, quietly looking out the window with her hands folded in her lap.

I have such mixed feelings. On the one hand, I feel sorry for her married to an old man and so far away from her family. On the other, I resent her for taking my mom's place, even if my mom bowed out at the end. One thing's for certain: she will never, ever be my stepmom.

My dad explains that he'd renamed his bride "Hanya" because it sounds like a warrior's name and includes a "y" like my sister's and my names. He thinks the letter "y" looks beautiful in cursive, and that's why we had "y's" in our names. I conclude that he sees her as one of his children.

His interactions with her are nothing short of bizarre. My dad boasts about how he made her cut her hair. She pulls out her wallet and silently hands me a picture of herself with long, beautiful, thick, dark hair. As I look more closely at her short hair, I can see the choppiness. I wonder if my dad cut her hair.

My dad says that her new haircut shapes the jawline of her face and explains that the nape is one of the sexiest parts of the human body. It strikes me that her haircut makes her look like a child. My dad's precise calculation in cutting her hair to make her look like a little girl makes me shudder and feel sick to my stomach.

Later that day, I run to the store, and Hanya joins me. She looks significantly younger than me, so I ask her how old she is.

She doesn't answer. She isn't talking at all.

"Are you okay?"

She quietly says, "Yes."

I don't wait to beat around the bush. "So, does my dad treats you well?"

"Yes, but he didn't buy me new clothes."

I wonder if she intentionally wore old clothes to get my sympathy—if my dad's joke held any truth. I think it's strange because the dad I know loves to give gifts. *Technically, I am her daughter. Does she expect me to take care of her and buy her new clothes?*

"In China, children take care of the elderly and their parents," she says.

Is she insinuating that I'm not taking proper care of my dad and possibly her? Feeling frustrated, I say, "I don't have that kind of relationship with my dad."

She hangs her head in response. Before returning home, Hanya discloses to me that she is 24. *She's six years younger than me.*

CHAPTER 11
AM I OK?

Shame is the most powerful, master emotion.
It's the fear that we're not good enough.
-Brene Brown

A s a single mother with two young children, including a special needs child, I'm determined to build a healthy life for myself and my kids. We have endured so much. My husband is gone, my mom has passed, my sister is far away, and my dad is emotionally non-existent. It's time to take care of myself so I can take care of my kids. I went to individual therapy while married, but I concentrated on marriage counseling and parenting a special needs child. Now I need therapy to heal from my traumatic childhood. I also need to know that I'm okay.

Initially, I battle preconceived notions that therapy is only for people whose lives are a mess, the rich, or the weak but I quickly learn that the purpose of therapy isn't just to treat an illness but is an excellent tool for enhancing well-being. I turn to therapy because I realize that I need another person's help to walk through the most difficult parts of my past so I can be the best possible mother, friend, sister, coworker, and partner.

Before going to therapy, I use techniques essential to my healing and maintaining the right mindset. I continue these techniques for the rest of my life. Aside from self-guided techniques, I embrace therapy with open arms. When I first seek therapy, I don't consistently have insurance to cover it, so I look for places that work on a sliding scale or accept my insurance. I go through Consejo, East Public Health, and Kindering Center, and I am referred to a few therapists. I vet them, avoiding ones who tend toward psychobabble, label me, or don't allow me to reach my own conclusions.

Every dollar I spend on therapy is hard-earned, and if I feel I don't connect with a therapist, I move on. My time matters because I'm paying for a sitter or asking a friend to watch my kids. Even the driving time is a factor, so I level with the therapist that I don't feel I can continue. I'm surprised when they aren't offended and help me look for the right fit.

Kathryn, my first long-term therapist specializes in parents with disabled children, and the therapy focuses on grief and loss. I like her because she accepts payments on a sliding scale; I can't afford therapy otherwise. She soon pivots to my repressed childhood memories, asking me to bring in family photo albums to help unveil the memories. I know where she wants to go, but I resist her approach because I don't want to go backward.

She suggests we do a timeline with the photo albums, starting with my teen years and moving backward to my toddler and baby years. She asks questions about my emotional state and how I coped. During one session, when I shared photos of me at nine, I came across a photo of me looking like a terror. I hold up the photo album to show her. "Oh, god. My dad wasn't the only one in the family with a dark side," I say, shame causing my face to flush. I set down the album next to me on the couch.

"What do you mean?" she asks, leaning forward.

I hide my face in my hands and shake my head.

"What's coming up for you? That's quite a visceral response."

"Let's see…How can I say this? I used to kick my dad in the balls," I flash an anxious grin, feeling awkward and exposed.

"You what?!" Kathryn's eyes widen.

"When I couldn't take any more arguing between my mom and dad, I'd get up, walk into the kitchen, kick him in the balls and say, 'Stop! Stop! Stop. I want everything to stop!' Sometimes I'd say, 'Don't you dare touch Mom.'"

"And what would your dad do?"

"He'd fall to the ground in pain. Although part of me felt guilty, another part of me felt good that he went down. But…"

"But what?"

"Well, then I felt so torn by guilt. I never felt good about it afterward. I would beat up on myself. Then I'd have the worst possible thought."

"Which was?"

"I'm becoming my father."

"From where you sit today, how do you see that little girl?" She asks.

I wonder what answer she's searching for. "Hurting. Angry. Wanting it to stop."

"What else do you see?"

123

I pause and reflect, and then grief and rage tear at my heart, unleashing decades of stored pain. I grab a wad of tissue from the Kleenex box and sob into the softness.

When my crying tapers off, Kathryn says, "Tell me about that."

I dab at my burning eyes. "I remember thinking, *You will never break me.*"

She nods. "Right. You were the strong one. You fought for your mom and sister. And yourself. Kicking him in the balls took guts, Cindy. You figured out how to stop the monster in his tracks. Do you see that?"

I nod. "I wanted to kill him."

"Of course, you did."

"I even grabbed a box of rat poison from the garage and sampled it to see if he'd detect it in his coffee. It looks like sugar but tastes bitter like chemicals. Does that make me an awful person? I mean," I hesitate, "maybe I got what I deserved."

"No, absolutely not. You were a child. You deserved none of it, not the physical abuse, not the emotional abuse, not the sexual abuse. None of it." She leans forward and holds my gaze. "Your father is a sick, sick man."

"But who wants to hurt another person?" I ask, still thinking it meant that I had an unfettered dark side.

"A person who has been hurt."

"So, is that why my dad hurt me—because he was hurt?"

"There's no way to know. But what he did was abhorrent, deviant, and violent. Nothing justified his behavior. And you had the courage to stand up to a grown man when you were just a child."

"Yeah, right around that time—when I was 10—the abuse stopped. I don't know if it was my developing into a young woman or my fighting back."

"Either way, kicking him in the balls was a genius move. I hope you can see that."

"Part of me can." Another memory surfaces. "When my dad had affairs with women overseas, my mom used to say with a smirk, 'Your dad won't be able to produce any more children because you've kicked him in the balls so many times.' That gave Mom true satisfaction."

"Yes, perhaps she wanted to do it but didn't have the courage."

I nod. It's bittersweet thinking about my mother living vicariously through me.

Kathryn and I have breakthrough moments and things progress nicely until a few months later I tell her about Spain. When I talk about sitting on the ledge, contemplating suicide, she looks surprised. She tells me that because of the way I handled it, I could potentially repeat the cycle and not tell anyone of my struggles. Each time we meet, she treats me as if I'm on suicide watch and asks roundabout questions about my safety and that of my children. I know she is doing her job, but I'm annoyed. I feel she's off track. I don't believe that because I had suicidal thoughts after discovering the truth about childhood, I'm at risk for suicide for the rest of my life. At 16, I didn't have the skills to talk to someone about my feelings or the therapeutic resources being in a foreign country with language barriers.

Sexual abuse trauma isn't one of her specialties, and she's way off in some of her observations and insights. When our sessions cause me anxiety, I conclude it's time to move on. I learn that when one struggles to resonate with a therapist, it's best to find another. Therapists are people too; they have their flaws and preconceived notions and factoring that in is important. No therapist has all the answers, but the right one helps in the quest to finding needed answers.

I eventually start seeing a couple offering Family Constellation or Pre-parenting Therapy. In this therapy, I'm grouped with people who've experienced a variety of traumas. A therapist couple leads the group. We select a specific trauma that a group member is dealing with, and the group reenacts the situation, but with a desired outcome instead of what really happened. If the reenactment isn't believable, we repeat the reenactment. The group must approve if they feel you are authentic in your process and really internalized the reenactment. Being real and authentic is the only way through this type of therapy, and all my emotions must be accounted for when doing a reenactment, which is called "your work."

I participate in this therapy twice a week. Even the reenactment of another's trauma teaches me valuable lessons. It's a very intense process. I continue this therapy for three years until I'm happy with my progress.

I find Pre-parenting Therapy, which leads me through intense—but extremely healing—sessions where I'm forced to face the deepest part of my childhood pain. This approach assumes we freeze at different stages of trauma. In Pre-parenting Therapy, two people role-play your parents and you rewrite the ending to a traumatic experience. For example, when I was a girl, I spilled my milk, which led to a shaming session with my dad. My mom cowered, and I cried and retreated to my room. In therapy, I rework the scene. The woman playing my mom says, "It's okay, honey. Don't worry about it," and she cleans up my mess. The man playing my father pours me another glass of milk and hugs me. The reenactment helps me find my power and voice as a child—one who's cradled by love and support.

After completing group therapy, I continue individual therapy. Because my upbringing was so chaotic due to my dad, I've lost the ability to be confident in who I am despite years of therapy. I want to make sure I don't have any underlying maladies or disorders and need an evaluation to bring clarity. I'm nervous, but I know I must do this for my peace of mind.

What if there's something wrong with me? What if I receive a serious mental illness diagnosis? What if there's no known cure?

I go to a psychologist and request a full mental health evaluation. After hours of questioning and testing, the psychologist looks up from his papers, steeples his hands, and says, "Cindy, here's my assessment. There's nothing wrong with you."

"Oh, thank goodness." I realize I've been holding my breath. I deeply exhale. *But then there's the issue of why.* "Well, why did I have so much happen in my life? I don't know anyone else who's had so many bad things happen."

He leans forward, looks at me intensely, and says, "Well, shit happens, Cindy. Some people have more. Some people have less. You just have more."

I laugh. "That's why you get the big bucks! Thank you." This resonates with me so much. I tell myself, "I'm okay, so start moving forward."

I vow to continue grief and loss therapy as well as deal with the post-traumatic stress from Brian's medical condition. I don't want to parent through the lens of grief.

CHAPTER 12
LIVING LIKE JOB

Adversity is like a strong wind. It tears away from us all but the things
that cannot be torn, so that we see ourselves as we really are.
-Arthur Golden

I often feel like Job from the Bible—tested in every area of my life. Not long after the divorce, my car is stolen while I'm at work, Brian continues to endure complicated surgeries, and I'm squeezed financially, emotionally, and spiritually. Yet, I find it ironic that, at my worst, I don't feel anger; I only feel love. I appreciate the things I have and embrace faith because that's all I have.

Eventually, we move out of our home in Issaquah to an apartment on Mercer Island, a nearby city. Despite the hurt from my marriage, I move closer to the kids' dad because I can't afford the gas to transport the kids back and forth; every dollar is accounted for. Before moving, I search surrounding cities to determine what free or reduced resources are available to me as a single parent. Their dad's city offers generous social services that aren't accessed by others because it is an affluent area.

My move is strategic; I anticipate all possible scenarios, as I can't predict Brian's health outcomes. Mercer Island is more central to Seattle Children's Hospital and has a school with a program for behavioral issues. Given that Brian exhibits behavioral issues from having his emotional center removed, I anticipate his need to attend. Mercer Island residents have access to Seattle Schools under special circumstances, and they have a signing school in Seattle. Brian is non-verbal due to the removal of his speech center.

I find a daycare with a sliding scale through the Stroum Jewish Community Center. Their staff members go above and beyond in assisting our family by offering camps, access to their food bank, and incredible emotional support.

To make ends meet, I piece together odd jobs. I occasionally housesit and nanny for families while they vacation. I clean offices after hours. I also clean a community hall and receive free Jazzercise in the compensation package, which is priceless! I sell Mary Kay products on the side from home, and I take any extra jobs that allow me to bring my kids.

Our complex, Shorewood Apartments is where many newly single-parent households get their foothold on the island. I connect with people coping with their shattered dreams, dreams of a lifetime of marital bliss borne on the altar of sacred vows. When "I dos" are exchanged with rings and a kiss, no one plans for this. No one plans for the acrid words, the betrayals, the frayed trust, the spiteful endings. It's an ugly, unknown, and heartbreaking process. It seemed much easier to pick up the pieces when I fell as a child but falling as an adult and picking up the pieces is complicated and unrehearsed. When I was young, I was in foreign territory and flying by the seat of my pants. This time, my flying skills are rusty, and I'm the captain. There is no co-pilot to man the controls if something goes wrong. It's risky to say the least.

Our apartment complex is undergoing a major renovation, so I work out an unbelievable deal on rent. We move from building to building, always the last tenant before a building is renovated. I'm able to reduce my rent sometimes to less than half. I do this for two years until all the buildings are remodeled. My kids play freely in the hallways; often, there are no other tenants in the building.

When we first move in, we have only the essentials. The living room is mostly empty with a few cushions on the floor. I also have a rocking chair in the living room that I sometimes rock the kids in, even though they barely fit in my lap. I've rocked them in this chair since birth, and it comforts us all. I have a kitchen table with four chairs and a time-out stool. The kitchen is the one room that's fully stocked because I love to cook. I have all my appliances and even a full set of china with daily dishes. The kitchen space is so full; its contents extend into boxes in the dining room. The kids share a room and have their beds and bedroom furniture along with their toys. I have a bed and a bedroom dresser. We have a TV that only gets local stations; we can't afford cable. Otherwise, our home is bare and echoes from emptiness.

Ironically, I'm living my mom's worst nightmare. I don't have my own home, a husband, or financial security. We have few material possessions and are incurring debt. We are isolated from our friends and neighbors, and I've uprooted the children from their school and friends. What Mom feared most was starting over again, which is exactly what I'm doing.

We are forced to give the family dog away when we move, and it breaks the kids' hearts. I feel horribly guilty and can't bring myself to tell them I gave him away to a neighbor. Instead, I tell them he ran away. The kids miss their home and playing in the backyard. Brian gets up in the middle of the night and sleeps by the door, anticipating playing outside, but there's no yard. They must get used to living in a smaller space. I'm stressed out financially and fearful about Brian's prognosis. I hate relying on the welfare system to provide for our basic needs, but I know it isn't forever.

Even though we're living simply, we have everything we need. There are several playgrounds in the complex for Brian to enjoy. Although Hannah misses her neighborhood friends, I reassure myself that she will make new ones. I know someday we will get another dog and make new memories. I remind myself that my married friends will always be there and that I need to establish single friends. Each time I go to a food bank, I think, *this is temporary; someday, I will be able to afford all my groceries.* If I embrace fear, I won't be able to live in the present, nor will I be able to envision the future. Sometimes, it is easy to see what we don't have, but I make a point to recognize that what we have is all we need. I say with confidence that the things we hope for in the future will happen for us.

I empathize with my children's losses when they're angry about all the changes.

Hannah asks so many questions: Where did our doggie go? Do you think he's happy? Why can't we get my favorite frosted cookies? Why can't I have new toys? Why can't we go to the movies? When is our next vacation?

I hang butcher paper on our bare walls and make dream lists for Hannah and me. Because Brian can't speak, she adds things to her list that she thinks he needs. Our dream lists are at least five feet long, and when Hannah asks for something, I add it to the list, asking her things like, "Why do you like this? What will you do with it? Where will you go with it?" It is a visualization exercise. Since Hannah can see herself with the things she hopes for, her urgent desire to have it at that moment diminishes. The more I believe in hope for our future, the more the kids believe in it, too.

Because our Christmas is so bleak, we focus on our wish list. We don't have money for a Christmas tree, so we make our own with two empty paper towel rolls and four toilet paper rolls. We tape them together for the stem and punch sporadic holes where we place foraged branches and twigs. We string popcorn, colored macaroni, and paper snowflakes to make a garland for the tree. We don't have Christmas tree lights, so I stick a lamp behind it and drape a colored scarf over it to create a moody glow. We surround the base of the tree with piles of books to hold up the tree. When I stand back to look at our creation, it has a slight tilt, but the kids are so proud of it! They even skip around our special tree.

The Boys and Girls Club graciously donates Christmas gifts to us. The presents are beautifully wrapped with sticky notes labeled "boy" or "girl." I have no idea what the gifts are. When Hannah unwraps her gift, she exclaims, "Boy, Santa got it all wrong this year!" She questions if Santa had the right address and if he got the letter she sent to the North Pole.

With our wish lists, homemade tree, and unmarked presents, it is truly one of my favorite Christmases. Watching the kids play with their new toys and listening to Christmas music playing on the radio, I am reminded of what I am grateful for.

Before my divorce, we spent a significant amount of money on medical bills. I called us the working poor. We didn't make enough money to pay our medical bills outright, but we made too much money to qualify for low-income services. Brian's first surgery was $1 million! In the first year of his life, the surgeries ranged from $40,000 to $90,000 because they were cutting-edge, and some of his medications were experimental. When Brian was diagnosed, I had private insurance, and after insurance covered their portion, I owed 20 percent of what remained. We quickly ran into debt.

When we divorced, my ex-husband declared bankruptcy, and I assumed the remaining debt because I was unsure if I could reestablish credit. I have two stacks of three-inch-high medical bills. I label one stack A and one stack B because I can't pay the entire stack. One month, I process pile A, and the next month, I work on pile B. I can't afford the cost of the check or postage if I attempt to pay all the bills every month. I go through a pile, and with each bill, I enclose an itemized statement explaining my financial situation that month. I include copies of child support if I receive any that month, the cost of my rent, utilities, and my income. I always include a check for what I can pay, even if it's only $10. I follow up with a phone call to ensure the recipient got my payment and letter. I do this for years and get to know my creditors well. After a couple of years, my medical bill creditors pardon my debt. With each pardon, I believe more in the humanity and kindness of people. I constantly pray and focus on what I have rather than what I don't have, which inspires me to keep a gratitude journal. At the end of the day, I write down my appreciation for a stranger's smile or a medical bill being pardoned. Despite the stress of my situation, I'm filled with love and gratitude.

Not long after my medical bills are cleared, Dad visits. He asks about my financial situation, specifically about my debt. I am relieved to tell him that the medical bills are cleared, but I say I still have a credit card debt and a car loan. When he asks me to show him the cards, I spread my 12 credit cards on the floor.

He asks about the balances and then randomly swoops up half the cards. "I've got these." Then pointing to the cards on the floor, he says, "You've got those."

He doesn't have to take on my debt. I feel grateful, and at the same time, I wonder, *is this what a normal dad does?* Once again, I face my internal conflict of loving and hating him. Just because he offers to help, it doesn't mean I can forget what he did to me.

As I look at him and think, after years of therapy, journaling, and thought processing, I still haven't been able to let it go completely. The struggle makes me realize I'm not done yet. I try to rationalize holding onto the past as a form of protection, but the truth is that I harbor deep-seated, painful memories that must be healed.

But this moment of protectiveness and generosity sparks the question. It's the question that pops up when I feel a moment of tenderness from him. I have a glimpse of what might have been. I don't always ask when it's on my tongue, but I do this time. "Dad?"

"Yes?"

"Why'd you abuse me as a child?"

The light drains from his eyes. He blinks dramatically like I've like I lost my mind. "I don't know what you're talking about. Why do you keep asking me the same question?"

"I need resolution. I'm trying to figure you out."

"I'm not the kind of person you can figure out, but I'm worried about you. Are you okay?"

I don't know what I'm looking for. It's almost like I have to prove to myself that he abused me. If he admits it, then I'll have the proof I need. But I let it go in silence.

This isn't the first time I've confronted my dad. I've questioned him many times, and each time he denies the abuse, it re-sparks my anger. His constant denial makes it nearly impossible for me to get the closure I desperately want.

At times, when I look at him, I feel pity. I know I'm walking through my pain, but I can't imagine the emotional weight he carries by believing his own lies. It makes me wonder how he lives with himself. Looking at pain rationally, I wonder if he is even capable of feeling remorse while in such deep denial.

When my dad assumes part of my credit card debt, the total combined amount is just $1,000, but to me, it's astronomical. I'm the main provider for Hannah, Brian, and me with a gross income of $17,000. I eventually earn more money and pay off the remainder of my credit cards and car loan debt. Brian's health improves, and with the clearance of my debt, I'm beginning to see the light at the end of a long, dark tunnel.

As a recipient of WIC services, I frequent the Public Health Department. I discuss with staff members my weekly updates on available community resources. Looking through the Yellow Pages for resources and communicating with medical debtors becomes a part-time job for survival. Local agencies eventually call me to find the most current community resources, and I become a reference for many agencies on where to find those resources. The Public Health Department creates a Resource Coordinator position focused on families with a special needs child. When the job opens, a friend in the department encourages me to apply. I hesitate because Brian has just completed epilepsy surgery. But after I learn it's possible to work part-time in the office and finish my work at home, I apply. I don't have a master's in social work, so they interview me 13 times to make sure I'm the right fit. I land the job, which is a continuum of my life. I feel perfectly prepared.

My work is rewarding, since helping struggling people find the resources they need is emotionally fulfilling. People say things they don't mean, and it doesn't faze me. Even if people say they don't like me, I never take it personally because I know they are at their lowest point. Since I was living a parallel life to my clients, nothing is surprising, and I'm able to empathize with their process. My role is to help low-income families connect with medical, legal, housing, educational, and state resources. Many of the skills I gained in therapy help me not take on their trauma; I can see and hear their stories without taking on the weight of their burdens.

I'm the first point of contact for families after their child has been diagnosed with a disability. I never know the condition of the home before I visit. I struggle most when I go into homes with hoarders or houses with animals not properly cared for. It is sensory overload. I habitually put Vick's Vapor Rub in my nose before home visits to mask the unbearable odors. My job is to help address their situations and connect their children with the appropriate resources. Inspiring families to make positive changes and escape vicious cycles is the most rewarding aspect of the job.

Given everything I've been through, I apply my knowledge and skills to my job. I share Brian's story with families and offer encouragement. I help families with new identities if they come from abusive backgrounds or flee to the US seeking asylum from heartbreaking situations in their home countries. I love working with a big team of public health nurses and doctors who have dedicated their lives to public service.

My kids love the social part of living at the Shorewood Apartments because they have built-in friends. I settle into a new normal with a satisfying job and new single friends. I'm out of debt, off state funding, and feel so much love and support from my friends. I enjoy decorating our home by making curtains, painting the walls, staining old wooden furniture, and entertaining guests in my small space. My children love their new school and new friends. I enjoy spending time with the single moms in our apartment complex while our children play. We talk over glasses of wine, swap dating stories, and laugh.

Despite feeling content, I wonder if I will ever totally heal from my past.

CHAPTER 13
COMING FORWARD

*These individuals are often extremely intelligent, charismatic,
and talented. Even people who know them well cannot conceive
that they are even capable of exploiting others sexually.
Such predators are masters of deceit.*
-Stanton E. Samenow, Ph.D.

A childhood friend from our neighborhood in Phoenix comes to stay with me. She has visited a few times since I moved back to the US. One evening, we're on the couch, sharing memories. She interrupts our reminiscing. "I have something to tell you. I've been carrying this around for so long." She doesn't wait for me to prompt her. "Your dad touched me."

I inhale sharply, feeling like I've been shot in the chest—a bullseye to my heart. We gaze at each other, her eyes burrowing into mine, her lips quivering. Tears stream down her cheeks and chin. When I pull her in for a hug, she releases her hold on herself and weeps uncontrollably—the kind of crying that might never end.

My eyes flood with tears, but I blink them back. This is her moment, not mine. As I fight the tears, my heart races. Heat rises in my cheeks as my stored shame surfaces once again. Although I know it isn't my fault, I feel responsible because he's my father.

She gazes at me after wiping away her tears. "I think about it every day of my life!" She tells me how difficult it was to tell her husband, and when she did, he wanted to kill my dad.

"How many times did it happen?"

"Only a few times," and she pauses, "but those few times impacted my whole life, my marriage, and my desire to bring children into this world. I mean, the thought of it happening to my children—not being able to protect them from monsters—is devastating."

My dad, the monster. I could hardly handle it.

"And it wasn't just me. Your dad tried to touch my older brother." Her brother is a few years older than me.

I shake my head with disgust. "I'm so sorry." I feel so guilty not only for what happened but because I wish I had better words to comfort her. I know "sorry" doesn't even come close to reaching the depths of her trauma. "He's a horrible man. I'm ashamed to call him my father. I know because it happened to me."

Her hands fly up to her mouth, her face frozen in contempt. "Even his own daughter. What a sicko!"

I want to share more of my experience but, plagued with guilt that my dad had abused her, I hold space for her.

We keep in contact, and I bring it up one other time, but it's clear she doesn't want to talk about it again. From my own experience, sometimes telling your story once or twice allows you to put it behind you.

Later that year, another girlfriend from my old neighborhood calls and says she has something to share with me.

I swallow hard and pray it's not another story about my dad, but I fear the worst.

Having her own children brought back memories. When she pauses, I wonder if she's crying. She describes a sleepover that should've been just girls giggling in their sleeping bags, eating candy and popcorn, and telling ghost stories—but things went terribly wrong. My dad turned it into his pedophile peep show. He offered her a dollar to see her breasts. Her voice is tinged with anger and disgust as she spits out the words "dirty old man!"

Shame about my dad rushes in. My face flushes. I marinate in disgrace—the spawn of such an awful human. I want to make it all better, take away the hurt, help her feel less shame, but I haven't been able to do that for myself, so how can I do it for someone else? I want to say so many things, but instead, I say, "I'm sorry. I'm so sorry. I wish I could take away your awful experience and the memories."

It takes courage for my friends to share their stories. There is something powerful in being heard. Some people must do it over and over to give their festering wounds a chance to heal each time they're exposed to light.

I never suspected that other people had been hurt by my dad, but after hearing my friends' stories, I think, *two people had the courage to tell me. How many other lives has he damaged?*

CHAPTER 14
LOVE'S BETTER THE
SECOND TIME AROUND

"I cannot remember exactly the first time your soul whispered to mine,
but I know you woke it. And it has never slept since."
-JM Storm

ark and I meet thirteen years before we marry. In the beginning, he blends into the background of my life. He and my ex-husband, Henry, were in the same fraternity and play on the same basketball team. Every time Mark and I run into each other, we have the same conversation—never graduating from pleasantries.

"Hi! How are you?" he asks.

"I'm good," I reply, not veering from our script.

"How's the family?" he says.

"Good," I say smiling politely.

After our greeting ritual, I make a beeline for the ladies, and Mark joins the guys. We do this for thirteen years, and I know nothing about him other than he is a good man according to mutual friends.

I hear through the grapevine he is a super nice guy, and he plays a killer offensive game of basketball, but I never give him any more thought.

When he is separating from his wife, we bump into each other at a bar in downtown Seattle. He's with some buddies, and I'm with girlfriends visiting from out of town.

Holding my cocktail, I speak loudly over the blaring music. "I'm so sorry. Divorce is a horrific thing to go through. It's the death of a dream and a life-altering experience." I shake my head, remembering.

For a second, I see him valiantly bracing against pain. His eyes squinted, and his jaw clenched. "Do you have any advice for a single guy like me?" he asks with a sly grin and sips his frothy beer. He momentarily has a froth mustache, which he licks away.

"Yes, definitely. Concentrate on your kids first. They won't like anybody you bring into their lives until they're grounded. Help them emotionally adjust to their new life. Also, get your financial house in order and clear your head as best you can before dating. Too many unsettled chaotic factors have the potential to bring down a new relationship."

"That's really great advice! Thank you!" He holds up his beer for a toast, and I clink my martini glass against his beer bottle.

"And the best part? It's free," I say, chuckling.

I enjoy our connection—helping a friend figure out the best path forward through a rough patch. If I had seen him as a potential date, I wouldn't have been as forthright in my approach; I would've used more finesse. I advise waiting six months to sort through everything before dating so he can be ready for a new relationship. I feel for his children. Mine struggled mightily when I divorced.

Later that year, he calls me, his name displaying on the caller ID: *Mark Benezra.*

Why is he calling me? Is he going to ask me out? We are connected through too many relationships. I know his ex-wife, and he knows my ex-husband. This is too close for comfort. I should pick up the phone to see what he wants.

We casually chat about light subjects, such as old friends. I still have an old-fashioned paper calendar that I flip through to figure out the last time we talked. *Exactly six months ago! Crazy!* I remember our conversation when I suggested that he wait for six months before dating. That's my rule of thumb, so it isn't hard to recall. My heart quickens, and I think, *no, it's not possible that he took my advice. Is it?*

Later, I learn that he had indeed waited for six months to the day to honor my advice and not scare me away.

"Would you like to have dinner and go to a concert with me? My treat!" he says with a lilt in his voice.

Oh, my goodness. "It's sweet of you to invite me, but I really shouldn't."

"Why not? I promise you'll have a good time. And, if not—if you find me a terrible bore, you can bail right after the concert." He laughs.

I glance at the blanket on my couch where I had been curled up, the empty box of Kleenex, the crunched-up tissues scattered on the floor from crying because my children were with their dad that weekend. *Quite the pity party!* I take my phone with the long-curled extension cord to the refrigerator. I wonder what I might fix for dinner if I stay home. I open the door to condiments, milk, a huge bag of string cheese for the kids, and leftovers. *This is pathetic. Why can't I go out?! Go and have a nice conversation with a friend. He's just a friend!*

After letting my guard down, I agree to meet him for dinner and a concert in Kirkland. As I swerve through the traffic, I think, *absolutely no kissing, just a friendly hug hello, and no flirting. He's wrong for you; you're a friend and that's all! This is just pizza and a concert, so it's okay to have fun.*

But fate has different plans. We have the most intense conversation punctuated by laughter, and we completely forget to go to the concert. Because I see him as a friend, I'm forthright in our conversation. He's unpolished because he hasn't dated in thirteen years. His approach is hilarious, and I giggle at the things that come out of his mouth, such as, "I heard I should play Usher on dates because its sexy." He asks me what I think about his parenting plan. Six and a half days with his kids, and a half day to date. He loves being an active dad, which I respect, but he's anxious to start dating and rebuilding his life.

"To be honest, I think it's horrific! It'll be difficult to date Ms. Right if you want to take her out for more than a few hours."

He asks hilarious questions: "Is chivalry really dead? How do you know when you've met Ms. Right? I chose Ms. Wrong the last time. How long do you have to wait before you sleep with someone these days? Then he grins, leans back with his hands behind his head, and says, 'I'm a catch.'"

My eyes widen. "You didn't really just say that. My advice: don't ever say that again to a date. Your ego's so big, how'd you get it through the door?!"

He pretends to punch me, and I feign exasperation. He's not smooth, but I'm amused. I tell him that he can be kind of harsh, and he tells me that I'm a bossy girl.

Neither of us has any airs. I've never encountered such genuine honesty. We laugh hard at our brutally honest exchanges. It's almost magical. There's no doubt he's charming, funny, and full of integrity, and he challenges my thinking in the most positive way. He admires me for all the adversities I've overcome rather than judging me for having had them. He respects the daily obstacles I face with my son's health, my handling of financial challenges, and the complications I have with my ex-husband.

For Mark, adversity is normal, and obstacles are something you work through, which speaks clearly to my heart language. We spend seven hours talking on our first date! It is magnetic! At the end of the evening, I give him a hug and a goodnight kiss on the cheek. I jump into my sexy minivan to drive home, and on the way, I take back everything I said while driving to meet him. I reflect on his chaotic life and his struggles with work and children, and I think about love. Love doesn't always come in a perfect package the way you hope. Love doesn't always match one's perfect checklist, and sometimes it comes when you're not looking for it. My checklist includes someone who likes nature, but Mark is a city boy.

When I ask, "Do you like to go camping?" he says, "No thanks. I'd never stay in a tent. I'm too old. There are rocks and bugs. I'll stay in a yurt. You know what I think? That you're a tree hugger."

"That's insulting. You can't say things like that." We laugh.

Even though Mark is a city slicker, I know he's the one for me. I think, *when you see love, go out and grab it!* I've been single for five years, and even though I fall hard for Mark, I fight it. Getting involved with him seems inappropriate because we know each other's exes. I also swore I would never date a newly separated person because of the potential emotional landmine. I already have so much on my plate with Brian's health, and I'm finally feeling confident in being single and on my own.

The following day, when I share my friend date with a grief therapist, who I'd never really clicked with, she shakes her head, purses her lips, and says, "Cindy, you're not ready for a relationship because you have too much going on with your son."

I feel the exact opposite. I've come to terms with my grief about Brian's health. I know I'll withstand a lifetime of losses as I watch him grow and not keep up with his peers. It is my responsibility to respectfully feel and let go, and I know I have the tools from years of therapy. It is time to apply them on my own. When our session ends, I give her a warm goodbye hug, knowing it will be our last.

Going against her advice, I call Mark and ask him out for a second date. It feels good to go with my gut!

We squeeze in dates despite his unfortunate parenting schedule. As we grow close quickly, I want him to know about the most painful parts of my life, including my sexual assault history. I really like him and don't want to get hurt if we break up over his feeling shame, embarrassment, or that my family and I are too complicated. By telling him early, I can more easily recover from a potential breakup because I won't be as emotionally invested. If I wait in fear to tell him years later, I'll put myself at emotional risk from a breakup if he's unable to handle my sexual abuse history.

Within the first month of dating, I risk sharing my darkest secrets. He has loads of questions, which I'm prepared for, but I did not anticipate his underlying assumptions.

He asks, "Well, if you were having nightmares or flashbacks about your dad doing this to you later in life, how do you know it's just not a dream? How do you know that this really happened to you?"

"Wow! I can't believe you asked me that." I'm stunned by his seeming insensitivity. They are fair questions, but it is irritating, nonetheless. I answer all his questions about my sexual abuse history.

"I have a relative with a similar history. Her family members were skeptical of her story, and it created an emotional stir in the family. Honestly, I wasn't sure what or whom to believe."

Can I date someone who would question the validity of an abused woman's story? There's so much evidence pointing to her abuser. I don't understand how he could have any doubts. I say, "It was a bold, brave move for her to share what happened. The fact that she went through so much family scrutiny and lost relationships over her deepest trauma must have been horrible. Can you imagine sharing your darkest fear only to have your family pull away from you when you most need their support?"

"Well, I haven't thought of it that way. So, how should I be when I meet your dad? I think I'm just going to take your lead. However you treat him, I will do the same. Is that okay?"

I'm comforted by his genuine response. "That would work. My relationship with my dad is really complicated, which makes me complicated, too."

I'm glad I risked sharing my past with Mark. Feeling vulnerable, I'm relieved that our conversation is over and am incredibly grateful for his support. This is the first of many conversations with Mark about my dad and the abuse, and it shows me that he is someone I can trust as a partner.

I try to put myself in Mark's shoes, and I know that I would want to know any sensitive issues sooner rather than later. If Mark had been arrested for something, had huge financial debt, had committed adultery in his last marriage, had a history with drugs and alcohol, or was a gambler, I would want to discuss those things early and get a chance to hear his thoughts. Sharing my story early opened the door for vulnerability and allows us to discuss any complications he had faced in the past.

He asks why I haven't shared my history about my dad with my children and if I ever would. He understands the emotional complexities of sharing with my children since they were so young. He understands why I keep strict boundaries with my dad and why I only allow him to come to occasional family dinners. Mark is thorough in his questions, and I'm relieved to see that my history isn't going to be an issue for him. He is loving, unbiased, and confident in my decision-making. I feel very vulnerable and emotionally raw afterward. I don't feel judged, nor do I feel shame, but I'm a little shaky because I had no idea how he would react.

Interestingly, it's my vulnerable state that creates more of a connection between us and a foundation for practicing honesty in conversations. In my first marriage, if we had hurt feelings, we didn't discuss them right away. Sometimes we would never address the issue, and by the time it came to light, it was ten times larger than it originally had been. When we were hurt, we moped around before we discussed the issue. It was a waste of valuable time, and I felt frustrated with myself that I was afraid to address any unresolved issue right away.

I don't want to bring my old habits into my new relationship with Mark. Brian is my constant reminder that life is short, and I may not have tomorrow, so living in the moment, even if difficult, is my new approach to life.

Tearing down old habits and not bringing them into my new relationship catapulted me into the hardest form of therapy I've ever experienced. Despite years of therapy, I still constantly question myself. *Am I okay? How does one know if they are emotionally healthy?* I know my family and friends will say I am, and that everything is going to be okay. But I need a professional to tell me one more time. I don't want one thing from my past to influence my behavior in this new relationship that I absolutely adore! I read that most remarriages with children were at a higher risk of failure because there are more variables. This scares me, too, so I need to dig a little further just to make sure I am emotionally healthy enough to cope with being a stepparent. It's all new and unexplored territory, and I need to look a little deeper and go outside my comfort zone to make sure I will be okay. I explore other types of therapy that aren't mainstream but are more tailored for my type of trauma.

When Mark and I discuss marriage in 2003, I return to therapy to make sure we're starting out on the right foot. We opt for group family therapy. Sometimes our sessions include one parent and one child, or two parents and one child, or just Mark and me. It's probably therapy overkill, but it helps me in every area of my life. I don't want to go into the marriage blind, harboring unseen complications. Therapy helps equip me with the tools to deal with our kids, our divorces, and even my job.

I want to make sure my kids are okay with me marrying Mark. I say to Hannah, "I don't have to do this if you don't want me to."

"Mom, are you kidding? I've never seen you this happy."

Three years after our first date, we plan to marry at the Salish Lodge where we have enjoyed hiking to the waterfall overlook.

Mark is the absolute love of my life, and I feel more than blessed to have found a partner who I call my best friend. I feel like I always strive to be better because he encourages me to be my best self. We have successfully blended our children into one family, which took years of intention and focus.

I've always taken parenting seriously, and I believe it's incredibly hard to be a present parent while also finding the balance to be with your partner and successfully work and find time for yourself. It's a tall order if we choose this lifestyle.

I work for the Department of Health until we marry, and then I consider leaving work and staying home with our four kids who need guidance and direction; we notice red flags in our teenagers' behavior that requires attention. It's tough to quit a job that I love where my colleagues adore me, especially when I come home and the kids ask, "Are you going to do this every day?" I've spent many years working with other people's children. It is time to completely focus on them, even though at times I feel unwanted.

Blending a large family takes diligence. We constantly establish house rules for teenagers with loads of emotions. They have rotating dietary restrictions. To make fewer waves, I cook what they want so we can eat together. I start a conversation with one child so their siblings can hear what is going on in their lives, seeing they didn't easily talk to each other. They invite their friends over, and sometimes we have up to ten kids at the table! I require everyone to sit down and use polite table manners. I cook family style, placing the prepared dishes on the table. If someone is late coming to dinner, they know they'll get leftovers.

We upgrade our car so six of us can fit into one vehicle. On our first trip, we reserve two hotel rooms in San Diego to connect everyone together in the same room. It costs a fortune for the hotel, food, and our activities. At the hotel, the kids jump from bed to bed, shrieking all the while. With the kids entertained, we decide to steal away to the lobby for a quick glass of wine.

As we're leaving, the kids ask to order room service. I think twice because we're on a budget, but they plead, "Mom, all we want is spaghetti!"

I shrug. *How expensive can spaghetti be?* "Okay, kids."

They jump up and down on the beds singing an impromptu spaghetti song that makes Mark and me crack up.

When we return to the room a half an hour later, three room service carts stand in the entryway. *If they only ordered spaghetti, why are there three carts?* On the table sit several large serving platters with domed tops. Hannah opens the top to reveal a plateful of lobster and crab on a bed of buttered pasta.

The kids cry, "Eww! Where's our spaghetti?!"

We glance at the bill. $75 per kid! Mark and I ditch our dinner plans and resigned to eat the meals they accidently ordered. Mark and I sit down to four seafood pasta entrées and the kids to the buttered pasta we added to the first order. That was a wakeup call for us; four kids have pack mentality, and we cannot leave them alone. Going forward, we will choose cheaper restaurants and will guide them with their ordering.

Hosting kids at our home is easier than going out to eat with so many kids and their crew of friends. We have a trampoline in the backyard the kids love, and often I walk in the entryway to find fifteen backpacks strewn about. Our two ovens are always going to feed the houseful of kids.

All the counseling really helps me with my kids during their teenage years. I pick three parental directives every day to say to each kid, one of which is emotional. Any more than that and kids tune out their parents litany of "make your bed," "do the dishes," "don't leave your shoes and socks in the family room." All the other things must go. The three things help me avoid being constantly negative. It can be a reminder to complete a task or a correct an action. I talk to them individually instead of calling them out as a group and shaming them in front of their siblings.

In my life, I am most proud of the relationships I have built with my husband and children. I know our strong family bond exists because considerable time and energy went into creating it. I know my parenting isn't everyone's style, but I never doubt it. I have complete confidence that I parent the best I can. I talk with my children as much as I can. I do what works for me, my husband, and each child. Communication is key in our family. The kids talk about everything; sometimes I find out more than I want to know, such as details about their sex lives that are TMI! Mark and I are open about the mistakes we made during childhood so the kids can learn from our mistakes and relate to us as people.

We are a family of talkers. It takes a long time for me to realize how much we talk and how quickly we talk about things. One time, Mark shares with me that he is disappointed in the way he handled a stressful situation, so we call a family breakfast that weekend. He apologizes to everyone for the way he handled stress by lashing out. He asks if anyone wants to respond to his apology. Two kids share their frustrations with his behavior and express hurt. Mark promises to listen more and weeps. My son-in-law, who recently married our daughter, says the breakfast is very unusual, and he doesn't have any words. We all laugh knowing that not every family is like ours.

The communication skills I learn in therapy are transformational in our marriage. We often pop into therapy for an hour session to get help with a specific situation. Eventually, we gain the skills needed to work through situations together. It's work, but the best kind of work.

Our years together have created a unique and special closeness. My family brings me the greatest joy, and I focus on them more than anything else in my life. When I look into the eyes of the children we raised together, I can confidently say they are good people. They are smart, fun, well-adjusted, and incredibly loving. If I were young, I would most definitely want to be their friends. I pat myself on the back and feel like my job to a degree is done. I remind my husband that we have remarkable children because they are good people, and that alone is something to celebrate. There is more love in this world just by them being in it.

I may not have been lucky in other parts of my life, but I have been lucky in love and in the family Mark and I created.

CHAPTER 15
DINNER WITH A PEDOPHILE

*"Be courageous and face this moment in time consciously
and with all the discernment and clarity within your power."*
-James O'Dea

My mother-in-law, Joyce, is curious about my relationship with my dad. She feels awkward having family
dinners when my dad doesn't attend. For special occasions, such as weddings, I say, "I'm not close to him." She says things
like, "Well, he is your dad, and he should be part of this, no matter
if you are close or not."

I wonder how long I can put off sharing my secrets with Joyce. But
as her questions and comments continue, I know it's time. Revealing
my painful past never gets easier. Whenever I anticipate sharing my
unthinkable trauma, my stomach clenches, and my heart flutters. I
feel breathless and lightheaded as if I were back there again. Back in
my childhood bedroom in Arizona, hiding under my covers, knowing the monsters weren't imaginary creatures hiding under my bed
but a very real father creeping around in the black of night. Then I

imagine inhaling the sweet, healing scent of the orange blossoms, and it gives me the strength to walk through the pain.

I sit down with Joyce over English Breakfast tea and chocolate croissants. We sip tea from her lovely China set, a wedding gift from long ago. The tea is so hot that I burn my tongue as if the words I'm about to share scorch my mouth before I've even spoken them.

"Joyce, I wanted to share with you something very personal, very painful, actually."

"What is it, dear?" she asks, blowing on her tea before sipping it.

"You know how you wonder why I don't always invite Dad to special occasions?"

"Yes."

"It's not that I'm an uncaring daughter. I thought you should know…he abused me physically, sexually, and emotionally when I was a young girl."

I don't know what to expect. I was so used to my mother making excuses for my dad. I half-expected her to do the same, but I'll never forget her response.

She bursts into tears and reaches for my hand across the table. "How can I help you with this? How can we help you through this?" Tears cascade down her cheeks. "I'm so terribly sorry you went through that." Her reaction is so loving and protective.

"Thank you, Joyce. It has been quite a painful journey, to say the least."

She mops her eyes and cheeks with a Kleenex. "For such a traumatic past, you seem really together."

I chuckle. "I try, but I don't always feel like I am."

Some people protect you, wanting to shield you from a person who's hurt you. Joyce helps me cope with the perpetrator who's still

158

in my life. Some may be annoyed by this, but I yearn for someone to show me how to navigate this thorny path. Her encouragement makes it easier. She is a wise soul—very much my teacher. I admire Joyce's strength emanating from self-love. She is well-spoken, loving, and fierce. She comes from a place of love and would die for her family. My mother was also incredibly loving, but in contrast to Joyce, I was the teacher when it came to facing fear. I have no resentment; it just makes me appreciate my mother-in-law's unique strength. She helps heal the part of me that yearns for a fiercely, protective mother.

For family dinners, Joyce asks if my dad will join us. Often, I plan not to include my dad, but she encourages me by saying, "Don't worry about me." She reminds me that I don't have to take care of her emotional well-being, and I can just worry about my own. I'm always concerned about other people's feelings about my dad being a pedophile that her simple words free me to look at myself and process my emotions with him in my space. Her encouragement frees me to decide based on what I feel is right instead of having to weigh everyone's opinions.

Every time we get together as a family, she leans toward me. "How are you doing?"

It's easy to be open with her. Sometimes I whisper, "I'm doing good," and other times, "I'm struggling." I know she's asking about my emotional state with my dad; she never has to say it explicitly. No matter my response, she encourages me. "You're a good daughter. You are doing the right thing."

Afterwards, she asks, "How was it for you?"

"I wasn't worried about you," I say.

"He really enjoyed himself."

"I can see you're becoming more settled with him. Maybe you can close some of those old parts of your life. You're going to be healthier for it."

My father-in-law is also very supportive of my coping with the messy process of having Dad in my life. He often pulls me in for a side hug, saying, "You're doing right by your dad. You are a good daughter, and I'm so proud of you." He then invites me for a drink. My in-laws' affirmations instill love instead of shame. They offer the priceless gift of unconditional love—something I've yearned for my whole life.

I integrate Dad into my new blended family of four kids with careful consideration. I assess every situation that includes him. I periodically invite him over for dinner with my children. I think having a grandparent in their life is important; they should know him on some level. I know I'm in control. I set the boundaries and leave no space for him to violate them. On many occasions, I confront my dad about the abuse, and it feels better to include him in my life with boundaries than pretend he doesn't exist.

Many people wonder why I choose to have Dad in my life. Having a sexual abuser in the family has so many layers of emotional complexity—love and hate locked in battle. Every time he denies what he did, the denial makes me feel crazy as if I fabricated the abuse. It's his word over mine. I resent having a dysfunctional family, and struggle for normalcy amongst the crazies. *I have a crazy dad, which makes crazy in the household,* I remind myself. Still, the love carries me through. I don't know. Sometimes, having my dad in my life feels like the right thing to do. Other times, I wonder because it's so much work and generates considerable grief. He makes me feel crazy like I made things up. I must prove to myself that these things happened. I want him to be accountable for his actions. I seek just two things: truth and accountability. Are those too much to ask?

It has been ingrained in me that blood is thicker than water—that one of the greatest things about life is the love of family. I feel this to be true. However, not all family members are healthy, nor are we always compatible. We don't choose our family; they just come with the package. Undeniably, I feel a bond with family, even if I don't care for or am irritated by them. To cut my dad out of my life would be more challenging than having him in my life, and it would weigh heavily on my conscience. To carry unresolved issues and not find some form of closure would be out of character for me. The best way to work through my issues and be true to myself is to have him in my life. My issues are so deep and layered around my dad that I've worked on them through the years and address them as they slowly unfold. If I don't do this, I'd deny who I am. I am, by nature, a person who seeks resolution and self-fulfillment, even if it's the harder path. This is not for everyone. It's what works for me, and I have peace and gratitude around the work I've done. People should find what works best for them. Ignore others' judgment because it's your path and the one you must live with.

When navigating conflict with family members, I have learned to hold them at arm's length until I can find a resolution or set healthy boundaries. They are all in my life on some level, and I believe it's harder to push that person out than deal with them. I don't delay issues because they are much harder to address if I wait too long; they become larger than the original issue.

I don't put much thought into conflict resolution with non-family members. If I get hurt by someone, I usually step away and later discuss the miscommunication if I'm vested in the person. If they do not have the skills or desire to resolve the conflict, I step out and let it be. I try to remember I did my best to find a middle ground and move forward. I seek peace and don't want to live with unnecessary turmoil. An individual may not resonate with everyone, and that's okay. It doesn't mean you are less loved; it just means you are "not that person's cup of tea," as my mother would say.

I hear Mark and Dad coming through the door and my stomach clenches. Dad stands at the doorway and looks happy to be here. I go over to him and briskly tap his arm, greeting him like someone I should care about. I feel like a fraud. Whenever my dad comes to our house for dinner, we have the same exchange.

My father is attracted to prepubescent children, and even though mine are teenagers or young adults, I still take precautions.

"Hi, Dad," I say. "Remember the rules. You're to stay at the dining room table or the bathroom—nowhere else. The children's rooms are absolutely off limits. Okay?"

His face falls as if hearing this for the first time. "Oh, Cindy, why do you have to be like that?"

"Those are my rules," I say firmly. It frustrates me that he acts as if he doesn't know why I set these restrictions. I remind myself why I allow my kids to know him.

"Dad, you made your choices. Now I'm making mine. Do you want to be here?"

"Of course, I do."

I gesture for him to come in.

Having dinners with Dad is a mental chore in two ways: first, coping with my emotional scars, and second, safely integrating my father into my family. Dad knows that I think it's a privilege for him to see his grandchildren, and he's on his best behavior.

Dad rarely had the opportunity to be around my kids when they were younger because he lived far away or out of state, and I had strict boundaries with him when he came to the house. Even though the kids are older, the rules are still the same. I reiterate these rules to him every time he visits, no matter how uncomfortable it is for the both of us. Dad is allowed to eat at the table in the main room and go to the bathroom. He is not allowed out of my sight.

A few weeks earlier, I told my mother-in-law and Mark that I think a few of the kids are old enough to learn that their grandfather is a sexual predator. I just need to find the right time to individually share with each child that I was sexually abused by their grandfather; every child deserves a one-on-one with me. They will react differently to the news because each has a unique perspective. My backup team is ready to support me. As soon as I feel that all the kids have the comprehensive depth to emotionally sort their feelings out, I will share. If one child learns the truth, the others will soon know, so timing is everything. I fear if I wait too long to tell them, they will resent me for not sharing. On the other hand, I fear that telling them will change their feelings for their grandfather and bring fear, anger, and shame into their world. I feel damned if I do, and damned if I don't. I remind myself that I have no room for secrets in my life.

Since we are in the same room, I'm hypervigilant, and my ears are perked for anything out of the ordinary. I listen to conversations, but I'm always listening elsewhere. Dad brings out my unresolved battle scars that therapists call triggers and I recognize that after all these years of therapy, there is still more work to be done. Will I ever find peace in my relationship with him?

It's a constant war I have within myself—the love-hate relationship I have with him. The reminder that given the choice, I can let go of the anger or hold onto it. My intuition tells me that I'm at my best when I resign to my true loving nature, no matter what my past held. It's easier for me to love, process, heal and go on than to hold onto the past. I have this mental struggle almost every time I see him. I want to let go but feel like I'm a traitor to myself if I do. Dad's my reminder of the dark and the light that lives within me and the scars that linger. I believe that if he admits the truth that he molested me, I can move on and heal completely.

I know that not all family members or friends can relate, or understand why I allow him in my life, but this is my mental dance. I'm worn out and have little space to explain my actions unless I am asked non-judgmentally. I find healing when I face my fears. It takes less energy to love than to hate; I know this because my body tells me so. That I have taken strict boundaries with dad, and we are safe. That I need loving support through this journey, not judgment. When I try to explain my process, it feels like people think it's too complicated and the best thing to do is cut him off. Maybe it's too hard for people to get on board with my reasoning because they wouldn't do it this way—but they aren't me.

With dad recently moved into a retirement center a few minutes away from me, I have so much more interaction with him. Often, it's daily. When Mark and I join dad for dinner at his apartment at the retirement home, I always sit next to Dad. At family dinners, nobody wants to sit next to him, and I don't want to burden anyone, so it has become a habit.

Halfway through dinner that night, Dad excuses himself to go to the bathroom. He goes to the kitchen cupboard and grabs a tall water glass and heads to the toilet.

Hmmm, that's an odd thing to do.

I get up from my seat and intercept him in the hallway. "Dad, why are you taking an empty drinking glass to the bathroom?"

Without making eye contact, he says, "Oh, I don't trust the toilet. I need to pee in the glass instead and will empty my urine into the sink."

"I can assure you that my toilet is safe." I reach for the water glass, and he reluctantly hands it over. I place it in the kitchen sink while he shuffles to the bathroom.

When he emerges, I'm waiting for him in the kitchen. I quickly scan the front of his pants to make sure he didn't urinate on himself. He struggles with incontinence and sometimes walks around with wet pants.

"Dad, what's up with going to the bathroom in a cup? And how long has this been going on?" I ask, hands on my hips.

"Oh, I don't know. I just feel safer going in a cup." He shrugs.

"What are you two doing in here?" Mark joins us in the kitchen as Dad scuffles past him and back to the table.

Speaking softly, I explain to Mark what happened. "I mean, I knew he was strange. What does he think will happen to his pee—alien confiscation?" I stifle my laughter by covering my mouth.

"Who the hell knows?" He whispers, "Here's what I'm wondering. Did we just drink water at his apartment yesterday from one of his kitchen glasses?"

I scrunch my face. "Yep, we sure did."

Because the kids have been through so much, I feel it's better for them to know my dad in a safe space. As adults, they can decide what kind of relationship they want with him. This is preferable to removing him from their lives as if he never existed.

I never take my eyes off my dad while he visits, and when he leaves, I ask the kids what they think of him. All the kids ask for seconds on dessert, and because they endured a dinner with my dad, I say yes.

While eating ice cream with sprinkles, my daughter Ellen says, "Opa makes me feel strange."

Brian waits his turn while enjoying a second chocolate sundae. He pipes in, "He's mean, Mom."

When I ask what he means, he explains that although he can never think of a time that Opa has been mean to him, he knows he's a mean person.

Michael savors his chocolate ice cream with whipped cream. "I mean, I love our intellectual discussions, but he does say bizarre things that make us all feel awkward."

While eating an ice cream bar, Hannah admits, "I love Opa because he's my grandfather, but he's really a sweet, weird person."

I appreciate the freedom the kids feel in expressing their spot-on perceptions about their grandfather and encourage them to listen to their intuition.

My dad wants to be included in holiday celebrations, and I have guilt about excluding him. He's grateful for the opportunity to be a part of our family dinners, but these celebrations leave me emotionally spent. I know it's a gift I want to give my dad, even though I pay a price.

I invite Dad for Christmas and Easter, as we celebrate those holidays with our immediate family. Christmas is especially tough because I see it as intimate—a time of cozying up with one another. I often find myself lost in joy and laughter, and then I turn and see him, and it is a painful reminder that I don't have the same freedom to be myself with him. Sometimes, when I enjoy a deep, satisfying laugh and he laughs with me, I feel I'm betraying myself. *Despite everything, it's okay to have a moment of laughter with him.*

Positioning him at the table for Christmas dinner is a challenge. I believe in keeping my enemies close, so he always sits next to me. No way would I let him sit next to others. Sitting next to me is a reminder that he must be on his best behavior. It helps me know where he is always, and I also don't want to burden anyone else. I resent having to go through the emotional dance with feelings that aren't my feelings aren't genuine. I smile at him when he talks to me and feel like an imposter. Pretenses on the outside, tension, and stress on the inside. And all the while wondering when he was going home, and I could have myself back.

Later, when he becomes a docile old man in a diaper, I try to remind myself that he is in a vulnerable life stage, and I have compassion for that.

Each year, I dread picking out Christmas and birthday gifts for my dad because it feels like a charade. I usually put a lot of thought and heart into gift giving, but thinking about what to give him only causes anxiety. I consult with Brian, my best problem-solver. He reminds what I gave my dad the year before and helps me pick out thoughtful gifts that don't require emotion, such as minced meats, jams, European cookies, cured meats, and port wine. Trader Joe's becomes the jackpot for gift shopping for my dad. The kids know I don't like my dad; they think he's weird. One year, Brian suggests feeding my dad small portions of food throughout the evening to keep his mouth busy so I don't have to listen to him! A brilliant plan!

In later years, my dad enjoys talking to our son Michael, who, as an adult, shares his love of intellectual discourse. Sometimes my dad wants to sit next to Michael to finish a conversation or start a new one. When I listen to them, the normalcy of it reminds me that they have an ordinary relationship—something I never had. Even without a history of abuse with my dad, I probably wouldn't have had long, deep conversations with him, as we are radically different people. When Michael and Dad are deep in conversation, I breathe a sigh of relief and slip out of the room. Reflecting on my dad's interactions with my kids, I realize that he's just another proud grandparent, even though he's mostly removed from their lives.

I have spent so much time and energy pushing abuse memories out of my mind. However, at times, when I look into my dad's eyes, there's a moment of recognition in which I know with certainty he remembers our past. In the flutter of knowing, I want to crawl out of my skin.

He says, "Oh, do you remember in Phoenix we had a symphony of crickets, and we'd listen to them on the porch? They would sing songs to you in the middle of the night."

Oh, trust me, dad, you don't want to go there. A lot more than crickets was going on at night. I held his gaze for a few seconds. "As a matter of fact, I do remember."

He looks away.

Those moments of knowing don't happen often, but when they do, I use humor to mentally remove myself. *Oh, this is what Christmas with a pedophile is like!*

I breathe and excuse myself to go to the bathroom. I close and lock the door, lean against the vanity, and gaze into my big chocolate-brown eyes, the ones that were closed when my dad woke me up in the middle of the night, the ones that looked up to him to be my protector, the ones that smiled for his midnight photo shoots, the ones that cried myself to sleep. Now they protect me from him, gauging his moves, and no longer look to him for anything. *Everything will be okay.*

Even though I focus so intently on my dad not taking my joy, I sometimes feel frustrated that I feel grumpy around him, questioning why I got stuck with a dad like him. For someone who hasn't been abused by a family member, it's hard to understand the emotional complexities of interacting with an abuser. I understand why people choose not to have that person around; it requires exhausting emotional and mental work. I also recognize that it is my choice to have in in my life. I'm not trying to punish myself or him. I hold him accountable for his words and actions, and because of that, I make space for him in my life.

When Mark and I married, I didn't invite my dad to our wedding. My aunt was unhappy about it, but I decided it was my day, and I didn't need to worry about her opinion. I decided not to invite my dad to the kids' bar mitzvahs and bat mitzvahs, and he didn't question it. For Hannah's engagement party and wedding, she and I agreed not to have him there. The wedding was a destination wedding, and my dad was ill, in addition to the emotional toll it would have taken by having him there. I wanted the day to be as stress-free as possible for her, and I wanted to be at ease. A few guests asked about my dad, and I just said, "Oh, he's too old," which wasn't a lie. I didn't even tell him about it. I planned that if he did find out, that I'd tell him the same thing I'd told him from the beginning: "I'm not trying to punish you, but this is the choice you made, and I'm reacting to it."

I don't invite Dad to family events that include extended family because some of his relatives struggle with facing him after learning about the abuse. I had recently told my cousin, and she said that if her dad, my dad's brother, would have known, he would have killed him. My dad never comments on not being invited to events; I believe he knows why. It's rare that anyone questions why he isn't there for large gatherings of friends and family. I don't want it to be uncomfortable for other families, and I have strict family boundaries for him anyway. My dad spent much of his life traveling and living an independent life, so no one expects him to be around.

My mother's family didn't learn about the abuse until she was gone. I delayed letting them know about the abuse out of self-love and to protect myself and my mom. I didn't want her punished or looked down upon. As a teen, I had many conversations with her about reaching out to her family to help us leave my dad. We discussed how each family member could help, but she had her reasons for not following through.

I didn't want her family to take the news personally and feel regret that they could have done something to prevent it or to help me. My closest aunt was devastated by the news and furious at Mom. "If I had known, I would've protected you," she said.

But that's what I was afraid of. Protecting us would've come at too great a price for my mom. In the end, I refused to take on their emotional grief about my mother and my childhood. It was theirs to carry.

After over 30 years of work in which I explored the reasons for Mom's responses, it's time to move on. I've resolved my disappointment with her for not protecting us the way I would have liked. My therapeutic work around her feels complete. I harbor no resentment and only have love for my mom, even with her shortcomings.

My dad is another story. I wonder if my healing journey will ever end.

CHAPTER 16
CERTIFIABLY CRAZY

"The mind is its own place and in itself,
can make a Heaven of Hell, a Hell of Heaven."
-John Milton

Mark and I periodically take short trips to Monterey, California, to visit my dad, where he's tucked away in a retirement community. On one visit, we plan to meet my dad at our hotel. As Mark, Brian, and I get close to the hotel, he says, "Is that your dad's car parked on the side of the road?"

"Huh? That's strange," I say.

"Hey—and isn't that your dad by the road?" said Mark.

"Oh, my goodness! What is he doing out here?" I ask.

Mark pulls into a space in the hotel parking lot. We jump out, hurrying toward a grassy ditch on the opposite side of the road from where my dad's car is parked. He's hunched down in a squatted position in the ditch.

Is he okay? "Dad, what the heck are you doing down there?" I ask.

With wide eyes, Dad says, "Big brother is watching us right now!"

Oh, so he is hiding. I'm frustrated and not that surprised. In a commanding tone, I say, "Dad, get out of the ditch!" *He's taking on a new form of crazy. This is going to be interesting.*

He doesn't fight back; he just stands up as if my command brings him out of a trance.

He glances at me and then at Mark and Brian and nonchalantly says, "Oh, hello!" He's wearing a pressed denim shirt, nice pants, and a belt.

"Opa sees UFOs. We're hoping they're going to take him," Brian says.

Mark and I can't help but crack up at Brian's candor. He always says what everyone else is thinking.

"No, really. They're out here," says Dad with wide eyes.

Mark greets my dad with a hug, and my dad warmly responds as if nothing strange happened, and the conversation normalizes. I'm shocked to see that my dad has a ponytail. His hair is all white and very thin on top, but he has grown a six-inch tail at his neckline pulled back in a rubber band.

We stroll into the hotel lobby and sit down, continuing to chat.

"So, Dad, I see you have a ponytail!"

"Do you like it? I blow dry my hair every day." He leans toward us and whispers, "I think the ladies like it! And guess what? I'm now a tango dancer!"

Mark, Brian, and I exchange skeptical glances. I doubt he's ever taken a tango class in his life. He had traveled to Argentina, so perhaps had seen enough to fake some tango moves.

"What would you do if you were invited onto the dance floor, Dad?"

He jumps up in the middle of the lobby and traces his right foot in a semi-circle on the ground, then his left foot. Moving his arms with an imaginary partner to replicate the tango, he says, "I'd dip her! Women love that!"

I cover my grin and suppress a huge giggle. I can see that he's serious, which worries me even more.

The three of us take my dad out for a fine dining experience that night with a view of Monterey Bay.

When we arrive at the hostess stand, Mark says, "Table for Benezra."

My dad chimes in. "Yes, table for four." Without skipping a beat, he doesn't wait for the hostesses' response and moves his left foot in a circular movement. Then he kicks his leg back into the air. He grabs his imaginary dance partner and makes a semi-circle with his right foot mimicking tango moves. He turns to the hostesses and proclaims, "I am a professional tango dancer!"

When Brian whispers, "Oh, we're crazy now."

I stifle my giggles.

A hostess smiles at him and says, "Oh, how interesting." The other hides a smirk.

My dad leans into me and says with his eyebrows raised, "See, the ladies love it!"

I can barely look at the hostesses out of embarrassment.

A hostess alerts us that our table is ready, but my dad is nowhere in sight. We walk into the main dining room to see an expansive window with sweeping views of the bay. Along the windows are intimate tables. The orange and golden light of the sunset sparkles and dances on the waves. As I scan the room for my dad, I see his back pressed against the window, his arms extended out like a snow angel. He's angled due to the slant of the windows and converses with a couple seated at a table, fully blocking their view.

"I'll let you handle it," says Mark, chuckling.

"Gee, thanks!" I say.

"I'm going with you. This is gonna be fun," says Brian.

We walk over to Dad, and I smile sheepishly at the couple. "Let's go, Dad. Our table's ready."

"How'd you get your hair up so high? Did you use pins or tease it?" my dad asks the woman.

"This is getting good," says Brian.

"I use hairpins," the woman says, giving my dad the side-eye.

My dad turns to me and says, "There she is," as if he had been looking for me. "Did you know she uses hairpins to keep her hair up like that?"

"Oh, really?"

"Her hair looks like cotton candy if you look through the light," says Brian ducking down.

"It does look like cotton candy," says Dad.

Oh, my goodness. I'm dying a thousand deaths.

"We're celebrating our anniversary," says the man through clenched teeth.

My dad clearly isn't getting the hint that they want him to leave.

"C'mon, Dad. Let's go." To the couple, I say, "Thank you for letting my dad interrupt your anniversary dinner," I say as a form of apology.

The woman says, "No problem." Relief washes over her face as we turn to leave.

We make our way to our table to find Mark has already ordered wine and appetizers. My dad admires the beauty of his wooden menu. After the waiter takes our orders, he attempts to collect the menus, but my dad refuses to hand his over. The waiter relents and walks away. My dad dominates the conversation with his conspiracy theories and how he's certain the government is watching us. During his incessant chatter, he manages to drink half a glass of wine, and then he politely excuses himself to go to the men's room. When entrées arrive, my dad has still not returned from the bathroom.

I take a huge swig of wine, hoping it will ease my pain. "Mark, I can't do this."

He kisses my cheek. "I know." He gets up to look for my dad.

I drink my wine in silence, gazing out at the water, wishing a sailboat would carry me away—forever.

Mark eventually comes back with my dad and jokes that he found him with new friends. Dad and Mark settle in at the table, and we eat our dinners in silence. I pray my dad has run out of nutso conspiracy theories. When the waiter returns to collect our plates and my dad's menu, he refuses again, having eaten his entire meal with the menu tucked underneath his arm.

Mark glances up at the waiter and shrugs. "I guess he's just enamored by your menu."

"You do understand it's property of the restaurant," the waiter says sternly.

"Oh, of course. We'll deal with it before we leave," promises Mark.

We order dessert, despite my already sending the signal to Mark to cut the dinner short.

Just before the dessert arrives, my dad walks off with the menu, which he refers to as a "food bible" in hand. By that time, the wait-staff is on alert, and a waitress brings my dad back to our table, saying in a light tone, "Look who I found!"

We finally make it to the end of the night, and he still refuses to return the menu. Granted, it is a beautiful hand-carved menu, but the absurdity of the situation is unreal—and to think this strange man is my father.

"C'mon, Dad, please give me the menu," I plead.

He hugs the menu to his chest and shakes his head like a petulant child.

I glance at Mark and mouth, *help!*

Mark springs into action and first tries to gently tug the menu from my dad's grasp. Dad resists. When Mark tries to take the menu by force, my dad yells, "He's trying to steal my menu!"

Oh my goodness!

When diners throughout the dining room turn to look at the commotion, I wish for an invisibility cloak.

After not getting him to part with it, we end up having to pay for it.

My dad is all smiles as he proudly carries his hard-won prize to the car.

That night, after we drop off my dad, I vent to Mark that my dad is at the peak of crazy. I tell him that I can only handle half a day more with my dad.

The next day is our last in Monterey, and we pick up Dad for a casual brunch. We park a block from the restaurant, and as we walk down the street towards the restaurant, my dad with startled eyes and a clenched jaw yells, "Get against the wall!"

I have no idea what's happening, so I listen and watch as he presses his back and hands against the outer wall of a restaurant like he's in a lineup. With terror in his voice, he says, "Mark shouldn't keep walking because there are UFOs at the end of the block."

I don't know why I go along with it, but I shout out to Mark to wait for us, so he stops at the corner. My dad continues with the madness, looking up to the sky. "I'm waiting for a UFO to pick me up. I'm ready to go."

Trying not to laugh, I ask, "Why would they choose you?"

He says with confidence, "I'm an interesting specimen, and they would want to study me."

His narcissism is unbelievable. I say sarcastically, "Yeah, you would be an interesting specimen. Where are the UFOs?" I kind of wish they would come and take him.

He points to the end of the block, where an elderly couple and some young people are crossing the street. There's nothing in the sky.

Fully convinced, he points to the sky and says, "Yeah, they are up there."

My mind races, and I tell him we need to go not to miss our reservation and lead him by the arm down the street.

At brunch, my dad is in a crabby mood and complains that we're leaving too soon. He's irritated about the coffee, then about the creamer. He goes from criticizing his coffee to criticizing me. "You took my grandkids away from me. You need to be taught…"

I don't hear the rest of the sentence because those words trigger my childhood abuse. He used that exact phrase when he wanted to control me.

Fury rises from my gut to my face, burning with rage. "Do you realize that no one else even visits you? You are certifiably crazy!"

I usually avoid these words because they trigger my dad, but today I go there. When I would call my dad crazy as a girl, he would come unglued and hurl whatever was in front of him—or worse, he would come after me.

"God damn it, Cindy!" He bangs the table, making the silverware dance. "Don't you ever call me crazy again!"

"You know what, Dad? I can't tolerate being shit on! From now on, I'm limiting our interactions to the phone." *Why am I doing this to myself? Because I don't want to completely abandon him. Who else does he have?* "Fine! What do I care?" He crosses his arms, squeezes his eyes closed, and sulks.

Mark and I leave that trip saying, "Goodbye," with a hug and a promise to call. One thing's for sure: my in-person visitations must end.

CHAPTER 17
RELOCATING DAD

"You can hide things from the world,
but you can never hide things from time."
-Kim Dong Hwa

We don't hear much from him or the nursing home staff for a few months. Then a nurse from the Monterey Hospital emergency room calls me ten times in five weeks to report that my dad is struggling with dementia and is unable to properly take his medication. He ends up in the ER with chest pain and shortness of breath after self-medicating with improper doses of prescription medication.

I speak with my dad on his tenth stay at the hospital.

He whispers into the phone, "These doctors are conspiring against me, so I've taken control of my medication." Dad yells after someone, "They're idiots!" His German accent is pronounced when he's angry. Again, he lowers his voice. "They absolutely don't know what they're doing. They're trying to kill me!" He slams his hand on what sounds like a metal tray.

I speak with the doctor about my dad's paranoid behaviors and learn that he hurls food at the nurses to keep them away, afraid he's being poisoned. The doctor shares that my dad swatted a nurse, and my mind races, fearing that he had swatted her butt. I'm relieved when he explains that my dad tried to prevent the nurse from touching his IV.

I ask the doctor to have my dad's mental health evaluated and suggest antipsychotics. I share with him that my dad had been on antipsychotics after displaying strange behaviors following his bypass surgery. I wonder who had taken him off the drugs. The doctor promises me that he will undergo an evaluation but explains in the meantime, my dad is being released from the hospital and sent to a state-funded nursing home since he was indigent.

I always knew this time would come, but I hadn't thought through the logistics. My dad is in the final stage of his life, and it is my job to make plans. *Why did he give me the power of attorney?* Probably because he knew I would always do the right thing, no matter the difficult challenges. I reflect on the last time I saw my dad. His outrageous behavior prompted me to stop visiting him. I kept in touch with occasional phone calls. Despite my efforts, our phone calls remind me of the past and cause more anxiety in my already stressful life.

My husband and I recently purchased a home in Kirkland, and we are going through a major remodel while mostly living in our home. It is not the fun and creative adventure I had imagined. In fact, it's the complete opposite! We're living out of suitcases and boxes, and at times, hotels. We raised a beautiful, blended family, and three of our kids are living on their own, but our eighteen-year-old son, Brian, still lives at home. Mark and I are helping him transition to college and independent living.

Brian is often incorrectly identified as being on the autism spectrum. He doesn't like to be touched, has tactile issues, hates loud noises, lacks social cues, and is cognitively brilliant in some areas but challenged in others. His sensitivities make our home remodel especially difficult for him. He despises change of any kind, especially to his daily routine. To have his meals made from a makeshift kitchen at unpredictable times, with a work crew banging away in the house, makes him extremely irritable. He yearns for a normal routine.

On top of the remodel, Brian's teachers encourage him to join the Transition Program, which teaches independent living skills and vocational skills to students ages 18-22, who receive special education services. Brian aspires to go to college after he graduates from high school, and the recommendation to join the Transition Program infuriates him.

I drive Brian to and from school every day; because of his seizure disorder, he can't drive. As we drive, he vents about how he feels patronized by his teachers when he voices his hopes of attending college.

One time, he blurts, "They all treat me like a retard, and I'm not retarded! They are! I hate my life!" He brushes his fingers through his shiny, dark brown hair as he does when he's stressed, and glares at me, waiting for my response.

I grab his hand, anticipating he will pull away in anger. We sit in silence a few seconds.

Feeling the tension in his hand lessen, I softly say, "I'm so sorry, honey. I can talk with your teacher."

With teary eyes, he pulls away to gaze out the window and calmly says, "No that's okay." A few minutes later, I once again extend my hand. He takes it but continues to look out the window. With Brian, fewer words are better. Action and affection mean everything.

Brian doesn't feel he has a disability; he instead thinks he has an *ability*. I agree and have always treated him that way despite his shortcomings. I like to remind him that he can do anything he sets his mind to. He may have to work a little harder at some things than most, but there's a workaround to any obstacle. Because I've so much adversity in my life, I understand him more than he knows.

Brian's brain tumor in utero triggered abnormal development. His facial bone structure is asymmetrical, and his smile is a little more turned up on the left side of his face. Also, when he's angry, one side of his face reddens more than the other. I only notice his unique facial features when he's upset. Another consequence of Brian's extensive procedures was an atrophied eye that became infected many times. The surgeons couldn't save his eye, so they removed it and replaced it with a glass eye when he was six years old. My boy has endured over 100 procedures in his lifetime!

Another time when I pick Brian up from school, he rants the minute he gets into the car. "I hate my teacher! You know what she does? She raises her voice at me so I can hear her better. Just because I have a glass eye doesn't mean I don't have ears. I can hear just fine! What's her problem?!" Even though Brian is visibly upset and angry, I can't help but laugh at the absurdity of his teacher's actions, which makes him chuckle as well. When he laughs, his wide grin feels like sunshine.

Though we laugh, I've never seen him like this. The frustration in his voice and the sorrow in his downcast, teary eyes as he peers out the window make me worry about him. Is he so despondent that he has suicidal thoughts? I later take him to a therapist to keep tabs on him. He resents me for doing this, but I don't know what suicidal red flags look like in a child with special needs. First and foremost, I want him to be safe. From the time of his diagnosis at four months old, I've never stopped worrying about him; he has always been a full-time job, but he is well worth the effort.

Despite the challenges with Brian, the news of my dad's failing health pushes him to the top of my priority list. It is apparent to Mark and me that I need to visit him soon. I sit down with my husband to devise a plan of action. He shines when it comes to strategizing. He's quick, removes all emotion from his decision-making, and thinks outside the box. We use humor to diffuse stress, and when we strategize, it feels like a quick game of mental volleyball, batting around ideas.

We decide that I will still go on my girls' trip to LA. I can't miss the Grammys! I'll leave early and meet Mark in Monterey to see my dad at the state-funded nursing home that he had been transferred to after his hospital stay. We decide that after he passes, I will transport his body to Washington since he wants to be buried in Queen Anne with the rest of the family. I made him a promise, and I feel obligated to carry out his wishes.

Mark sits in the hotel lobby, waiting for me to arrive. I'm so grateful that he moved his meetings, took time off work, and left all the craziness of our home life behind. When he glances up from his newspaper, his deep blue-green eyes twinkle, framed with happy lines. As he strolls over to greet me, I admire his well-put-together look on his tall, athletic build. I kiss him and feel his freshly cut hair on the back of his neck. He's thinning on top and keeps his hair shorter because, he says with a smile, it's less obvious that he's going bald. I silently acknowledge the privilege of growing old together. The thought of witnessing our changes over the years and deepening our love brings tears to my eyes. I recognize that the seasons we share are full of beauty and grace.

As my thoughts return to the present, I realize that there isn't anyone other than my husband with whom I'd rather make final arrangements for my dad. I know he'll always have my back and help me navigate the thorny path of death and dying.

As we walk through the doors at the nursing home, I'm overwhelmed by the stale odor of urine. I glance at Mark and pantomime plugging my nose.

The nursing home staff points us to my dad's room. When I push open the large wooden door, my eyes are immediately drawn to his bed. He's curled up in a fetal position on a thin mattress in a windbreaker and slippers, his back facing the door. His chest rises and falls steadily in sound sleep. He is oddly clutching a brown paper bag that I later learn contains his leather toiletry bag, address book, personal cards and letters in German, old pictures of our family, people and places I don't recognize, and a photo of him in scuba gear on the beach. His international scuba license is tucked in between the photos. These are his most cherished possessions, and he holds them close to his chest in the brown bag. Everywhere he goes in the nursing home, he's fearful that someone will steal them. I haven't seen him in a year and a half. He reminds me of a dying dog on the side of the road. *Should I just walk away? He won't even know I came. He'll live the rest of his days here. I'll consult with the medical team and create a plan for helping him remotely.* Frozen with indecision, I resist stepping closer to his bed. I need an escape plan if I decide to quietly slip out the door and out of his life for good. The longer I watch him in slumber, clutching his most cherished worldly possessions, the more I struggle with the idea of leaving without saying "hello" or "goodbye." My mind says, *RUN!* but the knowing in my body says, *stay.* I must be true to myself and do what's right for me. *I would help a dying dog even if it bit me.* I can't live with myself if I walk away. My heart sinks deep into my chest, and I reluctantly peer at Mark, which further grounds me in my decision. "I'm going to help him. I want to bring him back to Washington to pass away there."

Mark continues gazing at me, as if to say, *are you sure?* With trepidation, he says, "Okay, what is this going to look like?" I can sense his reluctance. He's probably thinking, *what the hell?! This man hurt you.*

We just stare at each other, conveying so much in our silence.

"We are going to pack up his household and fly him home," I say.

Mark's wide eyes look concerned as he reminds me that we are only in town for the weekend. Nonetheless, he agrees while rubbing his forehead. He suspects it will be okay and that things will work out, but he doesn't quite know where I'm going with it. That's Mark for you, rock-solid, compassionate, and feisty.

We speak in hushed tones to not awaken my dad. "We got this. We'll make it happen," I say, trying to convince myself.

I know it will be easier to bring my dad to a nursing home close to our house than flying back and forth from Washington to California. I need to be there for Brian, especially during this emotionally difficult time, and to be there for the remodel. I need to make daily decisions, like where I want my light switches and what color grout for tile. It's so trite compared to what is happening here, but I factor them into my decision. I also feel that if my dad passes away in Washington, it will be easier to keep my promise to bury him where he wished. It is mechanical practical decision-making, and it has everything to do with my needs more than anything else. In an emergency, I can always think calmly and quickly—a skill I acquired while resuscitating Brian when he had life-threatening seizures. Also, the serious medical complications from his surgeries required me to be calm, quick, and clear-headed, tabling my emotions for later.

I walk over to my dad and tap him on the shoulder. "Hi, Dad. It's me."

His eyes flutter open. Confused, he attempts to sit up, but he only has enough strength to lift his head an inch, and then he collapses back on the pillow. He opens his mouth and whispers something that sounds like "hello."

A nurse comes to his bedside to help us lift him into a wheelchair, and we wheel him to the cafeteria. The smell of the cafeteria isn't any better than that of the urine that permeated every part of the nursing home. The urine stench makes it hard to breathe, but I do my best to ignore it while I explain to my dad our plans for him and my reasoning—that I can't go back and forth and that I feel it is best to take him back to Washington.

He can't talk but nods as if he understands. I wonder if he has a sore throat or if he's just unaccustomed to talking. Growing up, we couldn't get him to stop jabbering, so I don't recognize this man.

He points toward the door, and his eager eyes say, *get me out of here!* with a nod and recognition that he is leaving soon.

I call Sonya that afternoon to tell her about my decision to bring Dad home.

"Oh, god, no! If you bring him here, I want nothing to do with him. Nothing!" Sonya sounds panicked.

"Okay, I understand. But can you at least write him once a month? He always asks how you're doing."

"I can try. I can certainly try. You just have to understand that seeing him is too difficult for me. It just stirs up so much stuff." "Tell me about it." I sigh. "Listen, I've gotta go clean out his apartment."

"Okay, Cin…"

"Yes?"

"Well, now I feel bad that you're taking this on. You also took on Mom when she was sick."

"No, you were right there with me, Sonya, when it came to Mom. I get it. Right now, your emotional bandwidth isn't there for Dad. It works for you, and I don't fault you. It's just what it is. Taking Dad on works for me. I'm doing this for me." I pause. "But can I call you and vent when I'm pulling my hair out?!"

We laugh.

"Yeah, anytime."

"Don't forget to send him a postcard or a letter."

"I know, I know. Love you! Bye."

That night, Mark and I sign the papers to release my dad from the state hospital, and then we head to his apartment in the retirement community to pack up his things. I have never been to his apartment, so I don't know what to expect. When we walk in, I'm horrified. It is a hoarder's paradise with odds and ends of furniture packed into the place. I remember my dad mentioning on the phone that when his friends from the retirement home would die, they gifted belongings to him. I thought it was sweet that he would have treasured keepsakes, but I had no idea to what extent his friends had done that. The walls are a patchwork quilt of random paintings and pictures of others, from the floor to the ceiling. There are little notes, on each frame, thanking my dad for his friendship. One says, *Hardy, I want to give this to you so that I can hang on your wall with your other friends.* Reading the notes feels like touring a memorial. Every shelf and corner are crammed with knickknacks. More letters from friends who had passed are scattered around. There's an organ in the corner with at least five ornate music stands nearby. It is like a cemetery of artifacts from old friends with notes of gratitude for his friendship. Mostly unfamiliar things fill the room, but as I glance at one corner, I spot his large wooden desk with etched gold florets still in perfect condition. I'm overtaken by a wave of shuddering fear. I heave a breath and childhood memories flood in—the feeling of terror and the pain of the punishments I received in front of that desk. Although it embodies my childhood memories, the desk is much smaller than I remembered. I imagine its final resting place—the dump—elated at the thought of it being crushed to splinters. I make a mental note to tackle clearing out the desk last.

When I stroll into the dimly lit kitchen, I find a filthy Vitamix caked with dried layers of food on the outside and notice he has been blending his food. He has a small pot on the stovetop half-full of stewed prunes. The prunes and the watery edges of the pot had a green and blue fuzz. The counters are sticky and cluttered with small bowls of partially eaten purees. I open his cupboards to find seven open jars of the same brand of peanut butter and two shelves filled with an assortment of nuts. All the bags have been opened, as if a squirrel had rummaged through them and left holes on all sides of the bags. On the counter, sit nine open identical bottles of wine. One drawer reveals hundreds of straws mixed in with sugar and ketchup packages, which I assume he had collected from different restaurants. When I open his refrigerator, I hold my mouth and nose and squint at the sight of rotten food in the far back, no longer in his reach, that had grown a thick fuzzy green coating like fine strands of hair. The sanitation, or lack of it, is revolting, and I hold my stomach to stave off nausea. In one corner of the refrigerator, four dozen eggs are stacked on top of each other. There's a slew of differently sized mason jars scattered about with stewed prunes and mystery blended food. Some jars of food are spoiled, and the lids were pushed up from the growing pressure of its rotten contents. He has hordes of bread, and the top shelf is filled with half-eaten jam jars, some without lids. There are spills that must have been there for months or longer. When I spot a jar of pickled vegetables sitting in a green milky mass, I dry heave. I hold my mouth and slam the refrigerator door to keep all the odors in. I rush out of the kitchen into the well-lit living room, wondering how his food hadn't made him seriously ill.

I grab a giant black garbage bag and head for the bathroom. As I walk in, I'm overpowered by a putrid stench of urine and mildew. I breathe out of my mouth, so I won't pass out. The sink and toilet have layers of scum in shades of pink and grey. The slow, leaky faucet left a clean spot revealing the original white of the sink. I navigate around all the gooey spots on the floor. I toss everything into the garbage bag as I go. His cupboards are packed with 30 to 40 packages of identical razors, volumes of shaving cream, and boxes of Q-tips. So far, in the scavenger hunt of my dad's life, I haven't come across much that stopped me in my tracks—but when I open the vanity drawer, I freeze. A bottle of Old Spice, my dad's signature scent, glares up at me. I nab it and quickly toss it into the plastic garbage bag, as if swiftly disposing of it can stop the feelings. Some cologne seeps out onto the counter and leaks onto my rubber gloves. The repulsive smell overtakes the urine and mildew, taking me back to the darkness of my bedroom when the scent preceded my dad creeping down the hallway. I could always smell him before I could see his skulking silhouette approaching me in the shadows.

Why am I bringing him back home? I can't even handle his cologne. This is all so crazy! Fighting back tears, I angrily shove the rest of his belongings into the bag until the bathroom is empty.

As I walk into the hallway, I notice stacks of *National Geographic* magazines on the floor and a curious trail of chunky dried-up mud leading from his bedroom to the bathroom. Bending down to gather the magazines, I catch a whiff of feces. I yell out to Mark, "Honey, Dad left a shit trail on the floor!"

He quickly appears in the hallway. "Too many prunes," he says, softly smiling. Mark has beads of sweat on his forehead and a red face from the exertion of cleaning.

"Honestly, I will never look at a prune the same way," I say, laughing. Grateful for a few minutes of comic relief, I continue sorting but mostly tossing stuff away.

When I walk into my dad's bedroom, I'm taken aback. While the rest of the apartment feels like a montage of friends' belongings, his room is distinctly his and much neater. The bedroom features his most cherished things. There were three big shelving units and a dresser. The large painting above his bed had hung in my parents' Arizona home. My dad always loved it because he liked to say he was like the old ship in the painting, sailing over stormy waters.

His shelves hold souvenirs collected from his travels. There are also framed pictures of my dad with my older half-sister, Christine, from Germany when she was a girl. Another shows her two children, Ann Christine and Stephanie, as little girls. Yet another large-framed photo captures Sonya, with her kids, Zach, and Sophia. There is a faded yellow card from my sister that says, "Best dad ever!" That is probably 20 years old. Nearby are many candid photos of my kids, Brian, Hannah, Ellen, and Michael, and my dad had framed them himself. Many more faces and places are pictured, including my mom and dad on their wedding day, my dad as a Boy Scout, my dad's childhood best friend, his mom and grandmother, Mark and me and my dad with a birthday cake, the entire family from Germany, me in my wedding dress standing next to my dad, my dad in his scuba gear, and my mom's relatives. There's even a picture of his ex-wife. In between the framed photos are childhood notes from my sister and me and cards from the grandkids. Letters from his German friends are meticulously folded and wrapped up. My childhood drawings are taped on the back of the shelf. It is like a shrine or offering place of his life, and all that is special to him.

Next, I rummage through his tighty-whitey and sock drawer, searching for scandalous things like pornography or anything insidious to confirm my assumptions that he hadn't changed. As I run my hands over the socks and squeezed every one of them, I feel hard objects inside them. I pull the socks apart and discover a small treasure trove of fine jewelry, including his graduation ring, his wedding rings from when he was married to my mom and to his second wife, and precious gemstone pieces. There are ruby earrings, a ruby necklace, several short, flat gold necklaces, and an emerald necklace. These are all wrapped nicely in cases, as if ready to gift to someone. My dad's love language is gifting, so I'm not surprised. Nothing seems out of the ordinary, nor is there anything incriminating. I'm quite relieved. Maybe he changed.

Pots of all sizes and shapes with dying plants and flowers cover the patio. I start cleaning there because it seems like the easiest place, but the patio alone takes several hours to clear out.

After the patio, we decide if we are to complete everything that weekend, we will need to hire someone to help us pack and dispose of things. We quickly find a moving company and a guy who wants to moonlight on the side. I tell him he can take anything he wants, but the desk must go to the dump. I say it has bad juju, and I don't want it going to anyone's home. He's grateful for the opportunity to make some cash on the side, and I'm thankful to see the house disappear. We work from room to room until all that remains is my dad's desk.

I stand in front of the desk, and my hands tremble as I open the drawers. I peer into drawer after drawer, carefully examining the contents, my fingers quickly sifting through documents, looking for something. I'm prepared to find something dirty or dark, but instead, I find religious materials. There are four different Bibles from pastors with handwritten notes. There are self-help books, such as the *Four Agreements*. He even has books about Eastern medicine and holistic practices. I had read most of the books and am shocked that he has chosen them for his reading library. He even has a Gua Sha, an ancient Chinese traditional medicinal tool primarily used to relieve muscle pain and tension. I'm stunned that he knows what that is. I dump out each drawer, faster and faster, but the things I expect to find are nowhere in sight. An odd feeling creeps over my body as I think, *I don't know this dad. I don't know this person.*

His computer sits on top of his desk, and I go directly into his cookies, hoping to find some answers, but his search history is filled with news and politics. Aside from financials, there is nothing out of the ordinary on the computer. Next to his desk hangs a detailed calendar filled with times for prayer sessions in the retirement home and organ performances for his fellow residents. My dad has never been religious. He was an altar boy in the Catholic Church and went to mass as a child, but I have no memory of him even speaking about God or any higher power. It is strange to discover that he now sought guidance from religious practitioners.

To see my dad's nostalgia for his family in his picture montage despite pushing everyone away, his spiritual books as if he were searching for something, the lack of incriminating evidence of pornography, and then to find out he attends prayer sessions; it's unbelievable on so many levels.

Everything is donated or taken by the mover except his organ, two guitars—which, oddly, are the only things dusted—a music stand, his photo albums, his sheet music, everything on his shelf in his bedroom, and a small pile of clothes. We ask a friend who lives nearby to ship his items to Seattle in a container. It's clear by the end of the weekend that my dad is not the same person he had been. He's malnourished, a chronic hoarder, who lives in poor sanitation and has mental health issues. I believe he has always suffered from mental illness, but he was never diagnosed, yet he's obviously struggling in his late 70s.

Between cleaning sessions, Mark miraculously finds an opening for my dad in a retirement center near our home that offers medical care. We fly back to Washington together. In just three days, we clean out my dad's apartment and make all the arrangements with the hospital and the new retirement center. It is a whirlwind, and we don't have time to stop and think about it.

Once in Seattle, Dad settles into a retirement center in Bellevue, and his health rapidly improves. He regains his strength and starts walking and talking again. A mental health team decides to keep him on antipsychotics at my request because he is anxious and sometimes has paranoid thoughts. On the medication, he seems happy, calm, clear-headed, and gentle—traits I have never witnessed in him. He is what I would call "normal." I get glimpses of the dad who has been trapped in Hardy's mind and body.

He takes medicine for his heart and receives excellent, consistent care. He starts to gain weight, and he even becomes so healthy that he can drive again. His drastic health improvement is so unexpected that I slowly come to accept that he's not going anywhere anytime soon. He starts to explore Seattle and the old neighborhoods he remembers. He does his own laundry and is particular about his grooming. He's no longer incontinent and takes care of his belongings. He requires nutritional support and management with his medications, but he seems to be a thriving old man. While I'm glad that my dad made a miraculous recovery, I think, *this was not the plan. He was supposed to pass away.*

I tell Brian that I feel confused about my feelings toward my dad. Brian sees the world differently, and because the emotional center of his brain was excised to remove his brain tumor, he says things without much emotion. He's very dry with a wicked sense of humor.

With a giant smile he says, "Opa (German for granddad) is like Rasputin. He keeps coming back. Just when you think he's passing, he will come back again—kind of like a cat with nine lives." He puts his arm around my shoulder, laughs, and continues, "Or maybe he has some unfinished business."

I haven't shared my history of abuse of my dad with Brian, but he knows that I don't care for my dad and wants little to do with him. His words make me feel uneasy and linger in my mind.

A year later, we finish our remodel and move into our home in Kirkland. We move my dad to a nice retirement center in the same city to be even closer. It is one block away from the water, so he took frequent walks around Lake Washington to take in the view. He'd walk to the French bakery coffee shop to enjoy his favorite danish and had his grandkids visit him when they could. He didn't have the opportunity to see them growing up because I felt uncomfortable about him being around them, so he was able to reconnect and know them as young adults. The retirement center had live entertainment a couple times a week and activities for the residents that he enjoyed. For the first time, I saw a completely lucid person. He seemed some-what normal. Because of his proximity, I was able to visit him every day, and caring for my dad became part of my routine. It was so sur-real to establish a normal relationship with my dad, this new dad I had never known before. I was still cautious and uneasy around him because I knew the truth of his past, but I felt like I was meeting a kinder, gentler dad I never knew—something I embraced in increments and with measure.

One day, I join my dad for breakfast in the retirement center's dining room. A pianist plays soothing music in the background, and the mood is light. I joke with him that it looks like he isn't going anywhere and that he got a second chance in life.

He says, "I know, I know, I never expected that you of all people would be here by my side. I remember that you said that I would be a very lonely old man if I didn't change my ways."

I shake my head, remembering the conversation.

"And look who's here right now."

I know what he's alluding to, but I can't believe he's even suggesting it. This is the closest he has ever come to talking about my childhood, so I seize the moment, fearing it might never come again.

"Why, Dad? Why did you do those things you did to me? I really need to know." I don't recognize my own voice. It's high-pitched, shaky, vulnerable, like that of a little girl.

I honestly don't expect a response different from his usual one, but that morning proves to be different. From the age of five until my 50s, every time I got my dad in a vulnerable moment, I would corner him and ask him why he did those things to me. He targeted me, and I never understood why someone would willingly hurt another person. He would glare at me as if I were delusional or speaking gibberish. He would tell me that I was making things up—that I had a fantasy about him. Sometimes he would pat my arm or back with fake sad eyes and artificial pity. I grew accustomed to his response but never stopped asking questions. I don't know how to let go of wondering what drives a person to destroy other people's lives.

How damaged is their soul? How do they rationalize their behaviors? Why won't they apologize to their victims? Damn the consequences! Do they not believe that the truth will set them free? I needed accountability to ease my pain. I needed answers.

I'm caught off guard when, instead of his normal reply, he says, "You were like a duck in the water." Continuing with that metaphor, he explains that no matter what the weather brought, I kept swimming and moving forward. He says that no matter what he did, it was like water running down my back.

Confused, yet still curious, I ask, "So you were trying to break a willful child?"

He says, "Yes!" while smiling, as if elated that I finally understand. He tells me that he resented me as a child and found me to be obstinate and resilient. He says he didn't have those qualities and he needed to "break me" of them.

The fact that he offered an explanation is unbelievable, but I try to make sense of his reasoning. My stomach is tight, adrenaline courses through my body, and I feel my heartbeat in my temples. It almost prevents me from hearing, so I take shallow breaths and periodically hold my breath to hear clearly. *Oh, he's sick. He's really ill. He's still that child on a playground. The biggest bully on the field. The most insecure and damaged of them all.* I lean in, wondering what will come out of his mouth next, and I can feel my eyes wider than usual. He is a true tyrant, as my mother had called him. I feel exhausted and drained by the little glimmer of truth he revealed.

A waitress comes over to take our order, interrupting our conversation. As quickly as he had revealed this lost secret, he shifts to talking about breakfast. "You have to have the eggs Benedict!"

In all these years, he never admitted or alluded to doing one harmful thing to me. He just said his mission was to break my will. To break the will of a child! His child! I sigh and think, *well, this willful child saved your butt and is paying for your eggs Benedict!*

The tips of my fingers and my toes tingle, on the verge of numbness, as often happens when I am scared. I wiggle my toes in my shoes to find grounding and covertly rub my fingers under the tablecloth to stay present. His analogy of me being a duck is an interesting one, and I can see that he didn't see me as his child, not even human, more as an animal. I rub my fingers on the edge of the tablecloth to feel something tactile and focus on the rich aroma of coffee in our mugs. I used these techniques as a girl to keep me grounded. *Stay present, clear-minded, and listen. Keep calm!* But how can I stay calm when my thoughts are shouting, *this is my moment of something true and honest coming from him! But be careful what you wish for.* I tell my thoughts to shut up. The volume in my head is deafening. I urge myself not to get lost in the crazy nuances of the scene. *Breathe it in, Cindy. This is his reality. This is his truth. This is how the truth gets dished up in life, even with eggs Benedict and hollandaise sauce. Take it or leave it.*

In my 50s, I'm introverted with extroverted tendencies. I have always liked privacy, especially when it comes to personal matters. When my dad shares this information, I know that I can't keep quiet anymore. It's time to break my silence, even if it brings discomfort to my family. I must share with others what I have learned from living a life with a parent who abuses you physically, sexually, and mentally. I must share my dad's thoughts in hopes that it might bring relief to others. It feels like I've been holding up a dam that I carefully built over the years to save myself, but the tiny bit of reality from my dad's mouth over breakfast poked a small hole in the structure. Suddenly, the pressure that held up the walls I had created is too great to hold up. I feel my truth will set me free. If I worked so hard to create the mental dam, then I could find a way to survive the flood that will follow. From that moment, I let the weight of the mental dam flow. It is time to be less quiet and private.

Filled with a sense of calm, I tell myself to have faith that I will find those who share my past. We will find each other and form a new tribe. Sharing my process can bring value to others. My story can provide healing. Fears set in as I think of being ridiculed by family, ostracized even, or shamed by others from telling my truth. It is a fleeting fear because, in my heart, I know I've chosen the longer road in life. It is the harder road, but it has always served me well. I assure myself that I will find the strength, as painful as it might be, to speak out for the first time. One does not have to scream the loudest to have a voice.

Sometimes quiet winds can move mountains.

Full of renewed strength, I watch as the kitchen staff clears our dishes. I look at my dad and ask if I can return and talk to him some more about me being a duck and his desire to break my will. I express my need to know more and thank him for being brave in sharing his truth. I take in his round, ruddy face, a small, unexpected smile. My eyes trace the etchings in his face and the large sunspots on his neck and arms.

With his hand, he carefully brushes the silver strands of his combover, laying them flat against his head. When he gazes at me with his deep blue eyes, he seems willing to share more of his truth. He pauses, taps me on the arm, and softly says, "Yes, my little girl, any-thing I can do to help you."

I want to burst into tears, but instead, I nod with appreciation. I tell him that I'll see him tomorrow, give him a light hug, and walk into the crisp Northwest air. Tears stream down my face as I search for my car. When I get in and slam the door, I rest my head on the steering wheel and cry until I can cry no more.

CHAPTER 18
DAD'S TIME TO TALK

"The only part of you that hurts when you're given the truth
is the part that lives on lies."
-Stefan Molyneux

Interviewing my dad marks the beginning of my publishing journey. I intend to write a book that will help others like me heal from sexual and physical abuse.

Our series of taped conversations spans six months. Toward the end, I decide to do one video. We meet in my dad's room at the retirement home.

"This will help other people, but the process won't be fun for us," I say. I wonder why he has agreed to speak about abusing me after so many years of denial. I can't help but ask, "Why now, Dad?"

"It's about time we talk about this," he says plainly.

I dig as deeply as I can, knowing this will likely be my last chance to get what I need from my dad. I breathe in strength and exhale trepidation. *You can do this, Cindy. You can do this.*

Me: "You know that I'm writing a book about our history, about what happened between us. Are you afraid of people knowing?"

Dad: "I'm not thinking about it."

Me: "You're not worried that people know about this?"

Dad: "No. It's the way it is. We were young, and God forgave us. You can write the details for the reader, and it will be exciting."

Me: "You think this will be exciting for readers to read?"

Dad: "Yes, if you write it that way."

Me: "So if I write it exciting, then readers will find it exciting. Is that right?"

Dad: "Yes."

Me: "Okay, so you just mentioned God. Do you believe in God?"

Dad: "Yes, of course."

Me: "Oh, you do. Do you believe God has forgiven you?"

Dad: "Yes, us."

Me: "You believe that God has forgiven you?"

Dad: "Us."

Me: "You believe he has forgiven what you have done to me? For what you have done to other people?"

Dad: "Well, yes."

Me: "You do, you do. Do you feel confident about that?"

Dad: "Oh, yes."

Me: "Do you believe that I have forgiven you?"

Dad: "That's up to you."

Me: "It is up to me, but do you believe that I have forgiven you?"

Dad: "Not when you go to work on it, and you go into details. It's whatever you like, but then you have not."

Me: "You believe that I have not. How does that make you feel?"

Dad: "It makes me sad. It's that way."

Me: "Did you ever think about that when you were doing these things?"

Dad: "No, it was mutual. I would say."

Me: "You feel that I wanted this to happen to me? That's what you mean by mutual?"

Dad: "Yes."

Me: "So, I wanted these things to happen to me?"

Dad: "They made you feel good, and that's mutual."

Me: "When I was little, when I was young, let's just make up a number, maybe five or six, and I didn't react, how could that be mutual?"

Dad: "Well, there wasn't anything when you were four or five or six or seven. There wasn't anything I had done with you."

Me: "So, you don't believe that you touched me when I was five, six, or seven?"

Dad: "No."

Me: "So, when do you think that you touched me?"

Dad: "When you were a big girl."

Me: "What would be a big girl?"

Dad: "Fully grown."

Me: "Fully grown?"

Dad: "You were a tall girl."

Me: "I was a tall girl?"

Dad: "And uh, you were constantly giggling and laughing with the other kids, together."

Me: "Would you say I was eight, nine, ten?"

Dad: "Ten. Yes, ten."

Me: "Do you think I was older than ten, maybe eleven?"

Dad: "Well, perhaps."

Me: "You once told me that you like the look of young girls during their puberty stage and young boys during their puberty stage, so I think you used the word 'budding,' when they were budding, blossoming."

Dad: "With young girls, you see them buttoning up, sprouting so to speak and that's a miracle of age. You see that kind of respectful, because you do not go and touch them to make sure that they are real."

Me: "So, do you get aroused by that? Is that exciting to you?"

Dad: "Exciting, it is."

Me: "It is? Why is that exciting?"

Dad: "It's not why. That's the way I'm built."

Me: "Dad, do you remember ever touching me inappropriately?"

Dad: "Oh, yes."

Me: "How old was I? Do you remember like any year or an age or a timeframe?"

Dad: "No."

Me: "When do you think was the first time?"

Dad: "The first time you were just there."

Me: "Touching me inappropriately. Do you remember the age?"

Dad: "No. You start growing up and then you start growing up. There is no timeframe."

Me: "So, I was maybe 5 or 6?"

Dad: "Well, that's 5 or 6, then you were 5 or 6."

Me: "Okay, and you remember that? You remember touching me then?"

Dad: "Well, then yes, because you are little. You are around."

Me: "So, then when I'm around, you mean because I was in the household, and I was physically around and playing around and always around in your space you mean?"

Dad: "Yes, you were in the space."

Dad: "I don't recall touching you, frankly."

Me: "I find it hard to believe that you can recall dates and can't remember touching me. I just almost find it next to impossible."

Dad: "You did not have a bosom, so there was feeling you. You were not built that way."

Me: "So, if I didn't have a bosom, did I have any hair on my vagina?"

Dad: "Well, you probably had, but then you don't move around without having pants on."

Me: "So, do you still feel that you touched me?"

Dad: "Well, you feel that I should recall it."

Me: "Do you feel that you touched me?"

Dad: "I should recall it, and then I don't."

Me: "Just a few minutes ago, you said you did touch me."

Dad: "Well, I don't recall that."

Me: "You don't recall just a few moments ago?"

Dad: "That I touched you?"

Me: "Yeah, in a sexual way. Horsing around? You don't remember any of that?"

Dad: "That could be. You were sporting the same way. You were hyper, and I don't know what you mean. Frankly, I don't know what you mean when you say touch. What was there to touch?"

Me: "Okay, so what was there to touch? So, when you would come in my bed at night and touch me in my privates. What was there to touch?"

Dad: "There was no private touching."

Me: "There was no private touching? You never touched me?"

Dad: "Not that I recall."

Me: "Not that you ever recall?"

Dad: "No."

Me: "There was no horsing around, or was there horsing around?"

Dad: "There was horsing around, but I know there was no touching you in your privates because there's nothing there."

Me: "Okay, so there was no touching but what do you consider horsing around?"

Dad: "Well, going to bed was always a hyper point that you girls got to sleep."

Me: "But what was horsing around other than going to bed and going to sleep? What does that mean to you?"

Dad: "Well, I was touching on your breasts, but they were little. You didn't have big breasts to feel and squeeze."

Me: "So why would you touch them if they weren't that big?"

Dad: "Well, that's the only way to find out how you were coming along."

Me: "To touch my breasts to see how I'm coming along...you can't see that?"

Dad: "Well, there wasn't much to see. There wasn't much to see. You'd have to have tight clothes on or something, but you were certainly hiding it."

Me: "So, the only way to see it was by touching me in my bed?"

Dad: "Yes. That was the time to touch. That was the proper time."

Me: "So, if you were to touch my vagina, my pee-pee as you termed it, was it just to see that I wasn't developed? Is that what it is?"

Dad: "Pretty much."

Me: "So, it was just to see?"

Dad: "You didn't have much to show."

Me: "And you were just checking to see, is that what that was?"

Dad: "Well, as you can say 'checking to see it.'"

Me: "What was it?"

Dad: "I don't recall going down, feeling you between your legs to feel. There wasn't anything to feel."

Me: "And you don't remember any of that?"

Dad: "No."

Me: "And what about when I was a big girl? Do you remember any of that?"

Dad: "What do you mean a big girl?"

Me: "You just said something about when I was a tall girl. Do you remember when I was a tall girl what were you doing then?"

Dad: "Well then, I probably would've touched you. But then touching is different whether you dwell on it or you just touch, and you get a reaction of it and you say no and that's their reaction."

Me: "So, when I said no, did that work?"

Dad: "Well, you didn't say no and that's no, and then that's opposite of saying that it's ok, but if it gives you pleasure that you were touched, then you can only answer yourself."

Me: "So, you still believe, it sounds like you never touched me now?"

Dad: "Well, I touched you, that's no denial, but for what kind of touching is there? Keeping hands on your vagina, that is casual touch."

Me: "Oh, casual touch, that is casual touch. Do you think sexual or physical abuse is about power or maybe educating somebody, or a sense of control? What would that be? What do you think?"

Dad: "Education. It's about time that they grow up and they feel it."

Me: "Oh, and you feel that as a dad that is something that you should show other people or show your daughters or other people?"

Dad: "I don't know what you mean about other people."

Me: "Okay, so as a dad that was something that you should educate your daughters?"

Dad: "Yes."

Me: "Okay. Do you ever recall educating, I'm using your word, educating any other children? My friends growing up?"

Dad: "Well, that's a different piece with other children. Other children, you don't when you say touch them, there's definitely a difference in means of touching. You go by them and touch them on the breasts, and they go like this (gestures blocking his chest) or laugh and the horseplay."

Me: "So, when you touched my friends on their breasts, did they have breasts?"

Dad: "Hardly."

Me: "But was that education for you or for them?"

Dad: "It's education for them because they are aware suddenly that they have something, and they are proud that they have a bra. That shows through the clothes or shows a button, and they are proud about it."

Me: "I see."

Dad: "Because now they are coming along."

Me: "So, it's education, and they feel proud of it. What if one of my friends wanted to have sex with you. What would you have done?"

Dad: "Well, there was none."

Me: "But what if, what if they said, 'Mr. Thomsik, I want to have sex with you,' or it led up to that moment—what would you do?"

Dad: "Well, it would be a nice surprise."

Me: "A nice surprise. Would you have wanted to do that with me?"

Dad: "No."

Me: "But someone else?"

Dad: "Someone else."

Me: "Now what would make you stop from doing it with me to somebody else."

Dad: "Well, because it had to stop because it got too far along."

Me: "You mean developmentally? Physically?"

Dad: "Physically."

I discover a new side to Dad. It's as if he's receiving daily shots of sodium pentothal or truth serum. My dad never openly admits to abusing me until we begin the interviews. He spent his entire life denying the abuse and pretending it never existed.

I'm taken aback by his ability to empathize because I've never seen it before. One time when we're driving together, someone cuts me off. I vent my frustration.

My dad taps me on the arm. "Hey, that's not healthy for you. You don't know what he has going on in his life."

I glance at him. *Who are you? Is there an alien in my car?*

UNDER THE ORANGE BLOSSOMS

He genuinely wants to know what my kids are doing—school, work, and even if they are happy. I didn't know he could be concerned about someone's happiness. I know the shift in him is because of the antipsychotics he's taking and being elderly, but no one could have prepared me for his transformation. He has become emotionally more stable and able to reflect, even though he's still in denial. This new dad triggers regret in me.

When I was a child, I remember seeing the words "manic-depressive" on an official-looking document. The term scared me. I asked Mom, "What's that?"

"Oh, it just means Dad gets sad sometimes."

I get sad sometimes. Does that mean I'm manic-depressive, too?

"Oh," I said.

Dad was mostly sad when lamenting travesties around the world. I'd wonder, *Why can't he feel those things for me?* He'd express concern for people in Africa without food or water and I'd wonder, *Why doesn't he have compassion for me?*

Now he says that I removed every stressor in his life, and he doesn't know what to do with himself. I suggest smiling, reading a book, or going for a walk. He has lost interest in keeping up with world affairs. For the first time, he enjoys the simple things in life; he focuses on the here and now.

After doing several audio interviews, I ask Dad if we can videotape an interview. He wonders why, and I explain. "When people see us, it will have a greater impact; they'll see our body language and our facial expressions." I explain that subtle nuances are more difficult to capture on audio.

"What are we going to talk about?" he asks.

"It will be like the audio interviews. We'll discuss your background, choices, behaviors, touching people in the neighborhood, and your legacy. We can skip or omit things as you wish. We can stop the video at any point; you just need to tell me."

"Will we do the interview before or after lunch?"

He's relieved that I say before lunch; he's worried about getting sleepy after.

"Oh, but what will I wear?" he asks, wringing his hands.

"Don't worry about that. I'll help you choose. Once we decide on your outfit, I'll take your shirt home to press it."

After admitting to the abuse during the audio interviews, my dad restrains and polishes himself during the video-recorded interviews. Whereas on audio, he seems raw and confessional, on video, he seems "on." As he begins to speak, my heart sinks. It reminds me of my childhood when my dad would be "on," and I could tell he was being fake. He's cordial to the videographer and seems proud during the interview. Even when he admits to touching other neighborhood kids, and he answers with a smile.

In the video interviews, he attempts a kind of apology for the first time ever. With tears in his eyes, he says, "I'm sorry I made you cry."

That's it? That's your apology? I'm enraged and throw my arms up in disbelief. I quickly remember that I'm doing an interview, and despite trembling with anger, I calm down and listen to his words. The words come to me: *I knew I wouldn't get the apology I needed to hear.*

I think, *He'll pass, and go with God now.*

He can't bring himself to utter, "I'm sorry," so I say, "No, I'm sorry." Why the hell would I apologize to him? I say, "I'm sorry" to convey that I feel sorry for him as a person. I'm sorry for the relationship we had. I say it because I know I can show full remorse, but he cannot. I find freedom and strength in it. It is so empowering. I knew he could spin it, deny it, say it didn't happen that way, but I move past it. I remember thinking, *I am in the power seat. I'm walking tall. This is not my shame; this is yours.* And in that way, I give him back the shame I had carried.

"I'm at the end of our interviews, Dad. I don't have any other questions to ask, and I know you don't want to be remembered by this, but these are my memories. Here's what you have given me. I learned how to stand up for myself. I've learned to speak my truth. I've learned to trust my gut. You were a good provider; we had a lovely home and a good education. I've learned how to work through obstacles. I will remember you for these things and for what happened in my childhood. I have let go of so much, though, in a healthy way."

The interviews play a huge part in my fully forgiving him. I give him the gift of being able to forgive himself. Because I forgive my dad, I'm able to forgive myself. I'm not to blame.

When I talk with sexual abuse survivors about forgiving their abuser, they share that such a thing is unthinkable! Some say that that is their ideal goal, but they don't know how to get there. Some forgave but found it to be a difficult process. In all my years of therapy, the idea of forgiveness has never come up.

Personally, I never sought out ways to forgive. I was more concerned about overcoming my PTSD symptoms, paying my bills, finding Mr. Right, being a parent, and seeking enjoyment. I didn't think past the recovery process, and felt I needed an apology from my dad to get the closure I needed.

I want to be free of the weight I carry at the mention of my dad's name. I realize I will never get the apology I need, so I write the apology I need to hear. I remove all the words that refer to my dad, so they are just my feelings expressing the apology.

I apologize for not being the father you wanted—for hurting my family and those around me. I was destructive to everything within my reach. Can you forgive me?

So many feelings rush to the surface, it brings me to tears—feelings that only make sense to me. I read it aloud over and over again. I gaze into the mirror, cry, and I say it until I believe it. It takes a few months to feel it in my body, heart, and soul.

I didn't realize how powerful forgiveness could be with a history like mine. I also didn't know that I had the power to heal myself. I didn't know you could be angry at times yet go through forgiveness in stages. I didn't realize that forgiveness is a personal process, especially if you have long-harbored resentment. It's like detoxing poison that has lodged in your heart, mind, and body. It cuts the connection to your loved one. It's not for the other person; it's for you, only you. It may take time but it's one of the greatest gifts you can give yourself. For a season, I daily reminded myself of the Mahatma Gandhi quote: "The weak can never forgive. Forgiveness is the attribute of the strong."

In the last year of his life, my dad is in and out of hospice. Every time it seems like he's about to pass, he rallies. The family jokes he has nine lives. I know I'm not going to get any more closure from him; that part of our journey has ended. It's out of character for me, and I feel shallow, but I just want him to pass already. The year drags on for an eternity, and I'm emotionally spent.

As an old man facing death, he has become more of a dad to me than at any other time in my life. He asks about the kids, especially Brian, what I'm doing, extended family, my health, and my relationship with Mark. I'm a daughter watching my dad go through his final life stage. Having already worked through my feelings, I'm able to just be with him.

Given the peace I've made with my dad, I wonder why, when I visit him once a week, I'm filled with dread. He's in hospice care at a new nursing home about 45 minutes from my house. I soon realize I'm not avoiding my dad, as much as I'm steering clear of the nursing home's owner. I find this to be ironic.

There are just four residents in the home, and the owner is also a caregiver. She's nurturing and competent; however, she appears to judge my interactions with Dad.

After my visits, she asks, "When will you come back? Why doesn't anybody else come visit him?"

I sigh, thinking, *I don't know! Ugh, I barely got here today!*

She knows nothing of my history, and I don't want to tell her. I consider it for a minute but conclude it's none of her business. Behaving endearingly toward my dad makes no sense. I've never had that kind of relationship with him, and I'm not going to start now. I also won't reveal our past because I don't want my history to affect the quality of his care.

One day when I visit Dad, he reclines in bed with his eyes closed. A chair and walker are parked next to his bed. The caregiver stands with her arms folded at the foot of his bed.

I plunk down onto the chair. "Hi, Dad!"

His eyes flutter open, and he attempts to sit up and move the blanket from his legs. He has forgotten he's too weak to do either thing.

I glance at the caregiver, thinking she'll help him. She glimpses at me with a furrowed brow and yanks the blanket back with great purpose. "Now that's how we treat the Papa. You know, he's the only male resident here, and he's very much like a Papa to me."

I cringe. *Ick! Should I share my history with her to explain why I'm so distant and unaffectionate?* I'm guilt-stricken for not having much compassion in his last stage of life. Then I try a familiar exercise to get me through that moment. I imagine inhaling strength and take several breaths to keep my composure. I think, *I have no shame for the way I react to my dad. Yes, people are aware of our strained relationship. This is the truth; now own it. Breath it out and move on!* I complete the meditation by saying, *Thank you for all your help with my dad.*

It's excruciating to witness a person dying, especially when it's a family member. It's as if the life force is slowly being squeezed out of the body in preparation for the flight of the spirit when the husk is left behind.

I don't have any ill wishes for my dad's death. I know I won't miss him, and, because of that, I'm able to bear witness to his final days without much emotion. He has a robust survival instinct, and I remind him it's okay to let go. I think about how much potential he wasted. He could've done so much more. Instead, he squandered his life and destroyed everything in his path. I wonder if he knows. Perhaps this was all he was capable of. I'll never know. I just hope that by sharing the truth with me, it brought him some peace.

The nursing staff is despondent they're losing Mr. Thomsik and ask if I'm okay. I can tell they wonder why I'm not falling to pieces. They probably think I'm in denial. Little do they know.

CHAPTER 19
THE DAD I ALWAYS WISHED FOR

"The life you have led doesn't need to be the only life you have."
-Anna Quindlen

W rapping up a visit with Dad, I glance around his room before leaving. Before he falls asleep, he says, "You are the last person I thought would ever be by my side." A recognition.

His face is frozen in anguish, his eyes pinched, and his breathing labored.

Dad's favorite painting of a ship in a storm is his sole decoration displayed on a sea of whitewashed walls. The ornate, golden frame contrasts with the dark, moody portrait. A beleaguered ship crests on a giant whitecap in a violent storm. A faint golden hue on the horizon hints at a possible break in the storm. I understand why the painting resonates with him—an embattled vessel at the mercy of overwhelming forces. As I slip away, I crack the door and pose the question I always ask when I walk away. *Will this be the last time I see him?*

I quietly leave for home to be with my family.

The call comes 24 hours later, and just like that, the man I called my father is gone, having died without friends or family by his side.

My mom predicted Dad would die alone. She would often say during fights, "You are going to die a lonely old man and all by yourself. I would not want to be you."

I always thought, *that sounds about right.*

I don't know what to feel because I've worked most of my life dealing with my feelings about him. I don't feel grief, but instead I hold deep feelings of resolution. He's gone, and I'm more than done. Without much pause, I tend to the funeral process.

The social worker at my dad's facility calls me, saying she's concerned that I'm having a hard time processing his death. I don't feel the need to explain. The truth is that I have a little anger. I do painstaking hours of therapy to uncover the truth and find a place for him in my life, to reach some kind of closure. There was satisfaction in taking care of him and being true to myself. Not living in fear and being authentic is what helped me move past it. Facing him head on is what I needed to do. This approach is not for everyone. I am settled. His abuse doesn't own me. I've taken my power back and now have insurmountable peace. I feel satisfied having worked through the emotional obstacles. I feel good that I was a loyal daughter.

For many years, Dad said he wanted his ashes scattered somewhere at sea, but as he lived out his final days, he changed his mind. He wished to be buried next to family. In the Jewish faith, we don't embalm, and we bury our deceased ones within three days. Although he wasn't Jewish, he asked to be buried this way.

There are two adjoining cemeteries on Capitol Hill in Seattle. One is open to people of all faiths and the other is a strictly Jewish cemetery. Mom is buried in the all-faiths section with family members, and our family plot is in the Jewish section with the previous generations. I've long imagined we're neighbors in the afterlife, stopping in for a chat or a happy hour.

I've always dreaded the thought of writing a eulogy for Dad because there's too much to say. I write it so quickly, so I don't have time to think. As I rehearse the eulogy in my bedroom, I wonder if it sounds callous. I take a break and head to the bathroom, notes in hand, and gaze into the mirror. *Should I lighten up? Should I only focus on the good things now that he's gone?* I look down at my favorite perfume on the counter and read aloud, "Jo Malone, Orange Blossom."

I don't change a word.

Dad,

Brian has some of the best sayings I know. About four years ago when we learned of your health, we thought your passing would be close and made plans for your final resting place. I recall Brian was with us on one of those visits, and he said to you, "Opa, can you die when it's not cold out? I don't want to be cold." Brian added that dying was very inconvenient and so was getting a cold. You smiled, Dad, and kindly said, "I will see what I can do for you."

For so many years, I used to stress over what I would say upon your passing. I'm not sure why I was so overly focused on this, or why it was a concern when you were alive and nowhere close to even being old, let alone passing.

But I now have a sense of what my apprehension was. As a daughter, I had a vision of what a dad should be in my mind and the possible feeling of what a daughter may feel toward her dad.

I really don't know these feelings. I only witness it when I see other people with their dads and what their bond of love looks like. I see it when my own children look at their dad and laugh, admire, fight, love, talk, and carry on.

I see it in movies, and I imagine what it would feel like to have that experience.

I'm always so incredibly happy for those who have a good dad. It's a beautiful thing.

This vision of what a dad should be like was not meant for me. This is not my story or any part of my life. I do have regrets, and I'm sad about this.

What I do know is that no parents are perfect. No one is. However, Dad, you came up short of my expectations of what a dad should be. I don't have any anger or hate toward you anymore. I feel sadder for the choices you made in life. I believe you did your best. However, your best was not good enough for me.

You did take pride in your family and provided for us financially with everything we could ask for and more. Education was a priority, and you made sure we got where we wanted to go. I always felt that in an emergency, no matter where I was in the world, I could call you and you would help me out. Like flying me back on a moment's notice if I got stuck in another country. When my car broke down in Canada, you drove four hours to fix my car on the side of the road and drove back home so I could continue to go on my vacation. Like picking me up from a strange party in the middle of the night where I lied to you and said I was at a friend's house. You didn't question me or get angry. You just came and helped me out.

I am grateful for that, and you have shown me how to take the unpredictable with grace.

As you got older and sick, I know we talked about legacy, about what you want people to remember you by.

You said you want people to remember you by your work accomplishments and how you took care of your family.

Dad, I do believe in the afterlife, and I also believe in reincarnation. I believe I had a contract with you in this life, and my contract is done. As a dutiful daughter, I can now rest my head on my pillow at night and know I did right by you until the end.

Not every memory of you is a poor one. There are lots of funny, quirky ones. I hope for my sake that I focus on those memories and find complete resolution on the ugly ones.

I wish for you that you have learned valuable lessons in this life.

I know I have already said this to you before, but if you do come back into this world again, I hope you have learned from the past. Don't make the same choices again. Bring only joy and love into this world next time, and to your life hereafter.

Be at peace, Dad.

Cindy

When it comes to making the funeral arrangements, Mark does most of the work, including choosing the coffin and headstone. I wanted as little to do with that part as possible. He calls me to tell me about the options for a coffin, the cheapest being a plain pine casket.

I say, "Put him in a pine box. It's good enough. Let's get this over with. Just share with the funeral director that he was an abusive father."

Later, Mark says the funeral director's comment was, "I assumed as much."

We honor dad's basic wishes, nothing more.

When the minister calls to plan the memorial service, I say that Sonya and I would like to read our eulogies. I add, "When you choose your reading, please avoid flowery or loving verses. My dad was an abusive man. It would be hypocritical to lay him to rest with verses painting him as a loving person." It feels freeing to speak the truth, one that was tucked away for so long.

"Oh, I understand. I know just the verse for your father's service. I'll just do a generic reading," says the minister.

"Thank you." No more lies. No more sacrificing myself for the sake of a broken man.

Everyone handles grief differently. After I read my eulogy, Sonya whispers, "Do you feel better saying that?" in a polite condemnation.

I think, *Yes, I do, thank you very much*, but I smile and let it go.

Sonya chooses to focus on the positive aspects of her relationship with Dad and celebrates him in her eulogy that she has everyone sign. It's a bit unusual, but I chalk it up to her quirkiness. She passes around his favorite chocolates during the funeral. My dad loved chocolate. Unwrapping and savoring the sweet delicacies while laying Dad to rest seems odd to me. I didn't want to honor him in that way, so I passed on the chocolate. Sonya placed small pieces of duct tape on the envelope of the eulogy to be buried with him, joking that he used duct tape on everything. My dad thought he could fix whatever was broken with duct tape and always had a roll of duct tape on hand. I'm amazed that my sister can approach his death with such grace given what I know now. When I told her about my book project over the phone, she revealed that Dad had touched her, too.

What? I had no idea! Why didn't you tell me until now? Had I said those words or just thought them?

"Cindy, are you still there?"

I guess I just thought them. "Yes, I'm still here. I don't know what to say other than I'm so sorry it happened to you, too."

"I know, but you had it so much worse. I feel stupid even saying anything."

"Sonya, please, no. It happened to you, too. Let's recognize that we were in this household together and shared the same experience to different degrees. It's still our pain.

His sexual abuse of my sister was brief, and she wasn't physically abused, nor was she the focus of his attention. It doesn't make her abuse any less important; she was still part of an awful environment. Two people from the same household can be affected by the same person and see him differently.

Sonya and I hold a simple funeral closed to everyone but our immediate families. First, Sonya and I read our eulogies. In the silence that follows, each family member places a white flower on Dad's plain pine coffin. We linger, huddled together, looking down upon the deep hole in the earth that would swallow him whole, dirt upon dirt, marked by a gravestone. In years to come, he would be overlooked as mourners delivered flowers, paying their respects to their beloveds. Some might stop, read his name, and wonder. *Who was this man? What was his legacy? Does anyone remember him?*

We stroll away from the gravesite in a supportive clump, having said our final goodbyes to the very flawed man most knew as

"Hardy," but whom we called "Dad" and "Opa." His chapter was over, marking the end of my dreams for a full apology in which he was remorseful and sought redemption, in which he transformed into the dad I had always wished for. It was too late for that. He was gone, along with my hopes for a real dad, the kind of dad who tucked his children in at night and kept the monsters at bay.

EPILOGUE
HEALING MYSELF

After leaving Arizona, I no longer visited the sanctuary of the orange groves because I had no memory of being abused until I was 17. However, when I lived in Iran from age 10-13, I found a familiar peace and stillness in the pistachio orchards.

Given my history, I have created grounding sanctuaries of peace and familiarity like the orchards. In all my homes, and even in my offices, I have set up spaces that delight my senses and recreate a grounding feeling.

I've created little grounding orchards within my home to feel connected to the earth by having my bare feet wiggle on soft textured rugs like the feeling of grass or cool textured tile like the damp earth below the orange tree. I have potted plants around the space where I can smell the damp soil. They bring in the beauty of nature and the healing color of green. They are the trees that wrapped me up like a blanket and cradled me in my grief. I place colored crystals, stones in trays or bowls within that space. I add mementos of dried flowers, sometimes pictures, handwritten notes, and gifts from loved ones to enhance the décor and magnify feelings of love. I place a scented candle within that space, different kinds of incense and things that can smudge and clear heavy thoughts within that sanctuary. There I rest and give thanks for the colorful journey of life.

I wear citrus-scented colognes, one of which is orange blossom. I go through my day with the scented reminder of the strength I found in the orchards. I find it uplifting and calming.

In our house in the desert, Mark surprised me by hanging a macrame hammock from Mexico. He tied it to orange trees in the backyard. The trees just happened to be the perfect distance apart. I like to steal away in the hammock in the late afternoon heat to read or take a nap. It fills my soul like no other space! I often close my eyes to listen to the birds' songs and take in the wind-scented orange blossoms that filter through the sturdy rustling green leaves. They sound like baby rattles when the wind filters through. I feel cocooned in the fold and sway of the hammock.

I now have my own orange orchard sanctuary in my backyard. I recreate my entry into this world with a new knowing to life with every nap. My past does not define me, but I have taken ways in which I have learned to heal myself. Drawing strength from sanctuaries has been a healing tool through which I have found growth in the colorful matrix of life.

Sharing my story has been a calling since I was a young adult, but I was never brave enough to step out in the open and boldly share with anyone who would listen. As a fearful teenager, I didn't want anyone to know that I was reading self-help books on abuse. I'd cover the outside of the book with adhesive wallpaper to hide the cover so no one knew the truth. Embarrassed, I'd steal away moments to read, but I never found the right book of inspiration. I became further traumatized by reading other people's stories on trauma which made me feel more isolated. It was so frustrating!

When my father opened up and acknowledged what he did, it was the fire that ignited my desire to share. I felt compelled to tell it all, even if others found it disturbing. It was as if the words, "Wake up, people. You need to know this happens all the time!" were blaring in my head.

This is the story I wish I could have found as a young person to instill hope and know there was light at the end of the tunnel. I hope this story will find those who have trudged through adversity. Know that you are not alone and that you possess the power to create the outcome you seek. Love and light.

SELF-HEALING TECHNIQUES

Over the years, I discovered self-healing techniques for my mind, body, and spirit that, along with therapy, facilitated my recovery. I turned to these techniques most often when I was hurting but sometimes even when I wasn't, I found them to be beneficial. I still practice many of these approaches today, as I view healing as a lifelong process.

Sticky Notes: One of the most helpful techniques that I use almost daily is writing phrases and quotes that speak to me on sticky notes. I place the sticky notes on my mirror, on my nightstand, in my drawer, on the refrigerator, and in my car. Any place in my home where I will see the note is a good place. When a quote or phrase no longer resonates, I put it away and replace it with a new one. I found that the bathroom mirror is a place that is most helpful for me so that I can say the quotes out loud while I look into the mirror. It gives me the chance to see myself accepting the words. I calmly say it and breathe it in. If something negative or trying comes up in my day, I find the sticky note with the quote that best helps me deal or move past that feeling. This practice helps me shift my thoughts from where they may wander and get stuck to where I need them to go to best support me.

I like to think about what that pile of sticky notes would look like if I put together the last thirty years of notes. It would be a huge blob of yellow, blue, green, and pink toothpaste-spattered sticky notes full of the inspiration and love that carried me through some of my toughest times.

For each person, the phrases that speak to them are different. These were some of my favorite phrases that have made the biggest impact:

"Choose the memories you want to keep." – When I am fixating on past traumatic events that I can't change, I attempt to remember the memories that serve me in the positive way to stop the negative chatter.

"Anger gets shit done. Use that anger and get it done." – When I recognize I'm feeling angry, I redirect my energy into productive activities. It could be completing a project, cleaning the house, cleaning a closet, cleaning the kitchen sink, reorganizing my closet, doing a workout, baking, drawing, or journaling.

"I am not about my struggles. I am about my achievements to overcome." – If I felt myself wallowing in self-pity, or when I would allow my grief to start to define me, I would remind myself of this phrase. I used it often when I started writing this book.

"Fuck judgment. Find your strength." – When I self-judge or when I feel judgment from others, instead I remember that I need to step into my power.

"Love is the only way through." – I say this phrase to myself every day, regardless of how I feel. It's my reminder that we struggle as human beings, but we are here and interconnected to love one another and loves ourselves. We must learn to forgive each other and ourselves, and love is the only way through. This is my constitution. It's part of my faith. This was a constant phrase that I used when watching my dad pass, and I felt that we were both coming full circle to each other.

Visionary Work: I have used visionary work since I was a little girl. I would imagine outcomes to situations. I would go into my room, close my eyes, and visualize the outcome I wanted to see or the outcome I wanted to feel. Later, I would rip out pictures from magazines or draw pictures and tape them onto an 11x7 piece of paper from my spiral notebook. Sometimes they were pictures of places I wanted to travel; sometimes they were words of how I wanted to feel; sometimes it was pictures of people showing emotions that I wanted to have; sometimes they were pictures of houses that I would want to live in, or décor that I liked. It was very much a vision board, but I didn't know that at the time. I would close my eyes, put the piece of paper on my chest, and envision those pictures and words on that paper happening to me until I felt a shift, like I believed it. I did this a lot with Brian's health. I would tear out a picture of a little boy playing in the grass and picture it and believe, even though Brian was in the hospital. I saved all my pictures and often, just before I would make my New Year's resolutions, I would take out all my pictures from that year and review them. I was always surprised at how many of them came true!

I also used visionary work to remove negative thoughts and feelings from my life. I would think of a particular phrase like "I hate you" and picture it in black lettering. If I was near water, I would take a shower or go for a swim, and if I wasn't, I would meditate and imagine water pouring down me. While the water was running down my body (either physically or in my imagination), I would watch the words slide down off my body, depart from me, and go down the drain. I often felt words or phrases were stuck on me, and it was a visual and mental strategy to cleanse myself from them. I began practicing this mental imagery when I was a teenager and still use this technique today.

Mantras: A mantra is often described as a statement or slogan repeated frequently. I use mantras to create an awareness in me. It is said to stimulate your endocrine system. No one told me to embrace mantras; I hadn't even heard of the word until adulthood, but I vividly remember telling myself as a young girl that if I kept saying a phrase, then I would believe it. My mom often told me that, "You are your thoughts," and I realized early that my thoughts had power. When I felt dirty as a child, I would turn to mantras to help me reject the feelings. I made a conscious effort to hold onto the memories I wanted to keep and let go of the ugliness. If something ugly popped up, I'd repeat several times over, "Choose the memories you want to keep," and concentrate on the ones I liked the most until I really felt the feelings of the memories I wanted to keep.

I used the mantra "I love myself and all my flaws, I love myself, I love you," when I struggled with depression and suicide. My sticky note with the mantra was a permanent fixture on my bathroom mirror so I would remind myself every time I washed my hands. Each time I saw the note, I would look in the mirror and force myself to say it twenty times.

As a teenager, when I was struggling with suicidal thoughts, I tried to find anything that I loved about myself to focus on. While looking at myself in the mirror, I would try to focus on my eyes and tell myself to smile. Sometimes it would mess me up because I would smile but not like my smile, and then I would have to start all over again. I would search to find things that I liked about myself. I liked my eyebrows, my front teeth, and the shape of my eyes. So, I would focus on those things because I really didn't like anything about my face. I didn't like my skin tone because my mother always told me it was too dark and that I needed to stay out of the sun; I didn't like my hair because it never did what I wanted; I didn't like my ears because they protruded; I didn't like the shape of my face because it was too round; I didn't like my high cheeks because they were too puffy, and somedays, I didn't even like my eyebrows. I spent a lot of time making faces in the mirror because it made me laugh. We didn't have cameras or iPhone filters to practice making faces with, so my sister and I would stand in front of the mirror laughing at each other's expressions. I didn't realize until much later how powerful my time in front of my mirror reciting mantras was to my well-being. At the time, it often felt so mechanical and forced, but I realize now how much my soul needed it.

Journaling: I have used journaling almost daily since I was a teenager as a form of therapy and self-reflection. Journaling has allowed me to express the raw, real feelings I have, which maybe no one else can or needs to hear. I've learned that every thought holds weight, but every thought doesn't have to be spoken out loud or acted on. Some thoughts should be discarded. Journaling helps me do this. It helps me filter my thoughts and hear myself without having to emotionally dump on someone.

There's something about writing my innermost thoughts on a piece of paper. The effort that goes into writing down my thoughts helps me realize and feel the weight of them in a way that talking about them or thinking about them cannot. At times, when my thoughts were intense, I'd write so hard that it would rip the paper. If the paper ripped, it felt like a natural release, and I'd throw it in the garbage. It was so freeing! It was like taking out the trash in my mind and dumping it in the garbage. I've thrown away ninety-nine percent of my writings. It often didn't make sense to go back and look at the journal entry again. I didn't want it to own me. But as much as I don't like to go back, it sometimes helps you to move forward. Therapy is very much like that. Journaling is a great form of mentally cleaning house. For the few journal entries that I kept, I'd reread them at a later point and either feel great that I had overcome the feeling or situation or realize that I hadn't moved past it—that I still needed to work on that area.

Exercise: From the days of biking to the orange blossoms, I learned very quickly that exercise helped me feel better and think clearer. In every season of my life, I try to squeeze in exercise. In some seasons, walks were all I could manage, and in others, I could commit to intense workouts, but moving my body in some form lifts my mood, my energy levels, and my sense of well-being. Being in nature, even if it's just having the window open, helps me realize that I am part of a bigger picture, and it is healing. Since childhood, I turned to swimming as a form of exercise. I find it to be true that exercise is just as important for your body as it is for your mind. A handful of studies have shown the benefit that spending even short periods of time outside before noon can greatly improve sleep and decrease feelings of depression. I believe that when our bodies move and connect to the earth, the benefits are greater than we know.

Self-Care: One of the simplest forms of therapy is self-care. In my most difficult times, I took care of myself by putting on my pajamas earlier in the evening, taking a hot bath, making comfort food, such as a grilled cheese sandwich, and turning on the TV and watching something funny. I was careful to not be overindulgent. If I was going to have a glass of wine or watch a TV show, I made sure that I stuck to one. It wasn't a binge session, and I was aware of how each action made me feel. I knew that overindulging would only backfire, so I made sure to savor whatever treat I allowed myself. Having self-restraint in self-care is very gratifying and powerful. I tried to be mindful and self-disciplined, and I often applied the same restraints I would put on my kids to myself. I would ask myself, *Would I let my kids eat the whole carton of ice cream? Would I let my kids sit on the couch for three hours and watch TV?* I used what I would allow for my kids as a sounding board for good parameters for myself to make sure that my self-care was really caring for myself and not wallowing in my feelings. Self-care never involved a lot of money because I didn't have the resources to splurge on myself. It was the action of putting time aside for myself to relax, rest, and enjoy something that I liked that took me a long way when my patience, hope, and energy ran thin.

Deep Breathing: I have utilized deep breathing throughout my life, and I still heavily rely on it as a tool to cope with daily stress. It doesn't cost a thing; you can do it anywhere, and it has immediate effects. There are many basic breathing exercises you can experiment with to see which one works best for you. My favorite breathing exercise is called alternate nostril breathing. The technique is highly effective for calming your mind in just a few minutes. It clears your head and helps with resetting. The technique starts with closing your right nostril with your thumb and breathing in four counts through your left nostril. Next, close the left nostril with the right ring finger. Briefly close both nostrils. Open your right nostril and breath out six counts. Breathe in the four counts through your right nostril. Repeat the technique on the left side.

Meditation: Meditation was another thing I did long before realizing what it was. When the sexual abuse was at its height, I would pick a color and visualize filling the room with that color. Sometimes I'd mentally surround myself in that color. It would help me rise out of my situation and take me somewhere beautiful. I'd often dream of champagne pink. I would imagine the pink color overtaking me and allowing me to float away from my current situation. At times, I would fall asleep lost in my meditative thoughts. These self-calming and coping practices naturally led me into meditation. After receiving formal meditation training, I realized that meditation was something available to everyone. Sometimes I would incorporate my meditation with an intent or prayer in that color. Colors played a huge part in my childhood meditation and continue to play a key role. I have gone through seasons with daily meditation and some seasons doing it sporadically, but it has always been a grounding practice for me. More recently, I took formal classes in meditation to help sharpen my ability to enter quickly into a meditative state. If meditation is new to you, there are some great, easy apps to help guide you.

Prayer: Praying and gratitude have helped me put things into perspective and acknowledge the things I can't change. Prayer evokes gratitude. It allows me to remember that even in the darkest days, that I have things to be thankful for, and because of that, I can live in a state of gratitude. Prayer shifts my focus from what I am lacking to the things that I do have and am grateful for. Praying helps me to shift the weight of "I have to do it all" to surrendering all my fears and worries to a higher power. It grounds me and helps me realize that I am here for a reason, that I am part of a bigger picture. My relationship with prayer is the longest relationship I have had. Prayer is a steady torch that stays lit no matter what is happening around me. It is part of my morning routine that I do in bed. I don't follow traditional written prayers, but each prayer involves asking for guidance and strength, asking for universal love, giving gratitude, and asking for health and safety for all people—especially for friends and loved ones.

Socializing: I have always enjoyed socializing and being in the company of others. During trying times, spending time, and laughing with a girlfriend is like medicine to my soul. It seems simple, but it is so healing. I've always felt fairly comfortable in whatever group I was in. I never felt that I needed to be the funniest, prettiest, most popular, smartest, or loudest, and so it made socializing easy for me. I felt fiercely independent and didn't feel threatened to have to be someone other than myself. Being friendly to others came naturally and helped me fit in anywhere, but I also made a point to be open to accepting others and not worrying if I wasn't accepted in return. As I've matured, I'm most comfortable in smaller crowds. I find it more meaningful and easier to connect deeper with people with less distraction. Moments laughing with close friends create lasting memories that sustain me.

Reike: Reike is a healing technique based on the idea that a therapist can channel energy to a person using touch to help activate natural healing. I have had the privilege of working with a Reike master who has not only helped me but other family members as well. Often, my Reike sessions consisted of me casually talking to her about my day, and she would place her hands in a series of positions over or slightly above my body. She always seemed to tap into something that I was struggling with emotionally; she would feel it and sense it energetically. It is helpful in promoting healing by activation response and helping the body find balance. It is especially helpful with my son Brian. Due to his brain tumor, he is missing an emotional center in his brain. The sessions have helped ground him.

Creative Projects: I have always valued art and began using art as a form of release, early in life. With my kids, I used art as a form of release. Art with my kids was simple and therapeutic. Often, we would do art projects that involved gluing whatever we had. Sometimes it was just two kinds of beans and macaroni, but there was something powerful and releasing about creating something. I found it especially important to find ways to release and cope with my emotions in the house with kids; getting away when they were young was not always possible. These techniques became a large part of my life out of necessity to mentally make it through each day.

As a child, I enjoyed coloring and drawing as a creative outlet. As a teenager, I loved to decorate my bedroom or bake and decorate cakes.

As an adult, when I felt I needed a mental refresh, I would decorate my living space in different ways with furniture I owned. The challenge of recreating a space using only what I had was rewarding. Sometimes I would bring in new, small items to give it a reboot and a fresh look.

Likewise, creating a beautiful meal, decorating the table, and eating in a beautiful setting was therapeutic. It brought togetherness and laughter with family and friends. When I cook, I picture throwing bits of love into my cooking, and I imagine my family and friends taking bites of love that I had tossed into my dishes. Creative gratification has been an outlet that has served me well.

ACKNOWLEDGMENT

All my love and gratitude to my best friend, and husband Mark Benezra. My remarkable children Brian, Paul, Michael, Ellen and Hannah. You are my world and the light of my life!

Sonya French, little sister. I will always hold your hand across any road. Thank you for sharing the precious bond of sisterhood.

Elizabeth Agemotu, Editor/Writer. Thank you for nurturing me through the inception of thought in creating this book to the end. You gathered up the pieces of my life to get them on paper. You're an unstoppable force that stood by my side for five years. What an earth angel.

Ann Tinkham, Writer, Mark Graham Communications. Thank you for molding my voice and making me show up in this world. I gained not only skills from you, but a beautiful friendship as well.

Colin Graham, Book Design, Graham Publishing Group. Thank you for taking care of the endless details in creating this book and the outstanding cover.

Angela Schellenberg, Counseling/Coaching. Thank you for being tough, real, and loving. You showed me different levels of healing and growth that I did not know was possible. Forever grateful.

Betty Globa, Photogrpaher. Through your lenses you make this world and everyone in it look magical. You are such a blessing.

Jeannette Igtanloc, Stylist. My life may not be perfect, but my hair is. Thank you.

Incredibly grateful to the 43 friends and family members that spent the time to read through a raw manuscript. Your feedback was priceless. Thank you, I couldn't have done this without you.

Yolanda G., Cyndi H.,Wendy H., Sonya F., Angie B., Tony R., Gayle K., Marcia E., Paul M., Dagmar T., Nanci M., Mark B., Beth C., Julie I., Jami B., Lesley P., Stephanie M., Courtney P., Deven B., Elizabeth A., Lori L., Mike S., Elaina P., Mark A., Shal F., Mary H., Chris A., Dana F., Susan K., Sheila O., Fredda G., Michele K., Shay F., Cati A., Sarah M., Val P., Katerie S., Stephanie S., Nancy G., Mandy M., Tracey L., Shari L., Trish M.

Cindy Benezra, *is a successful luxury event planner and philanthropist. She lives in Seattle with her husband and together they have four adult children. Aside from planning, she has written her heartfelt story for the first time.*

You can find more information at www.cindytalks.com.

CPSIA information can be obtained
at www.ICGtesting.com
Printed in the USA
LVHW010247020422
714934LV00010B/1121